TUTORING ADOLESCENT LITERACY LEARNERS

Solving Problems in the Teaching of Literacy
Cathy Collins Block, *Series Editor*

Recent volumes

TUTORING ADOLESCENT LITERACY LEARNERS

A Guide for Volunteers

KELLY CHANDLER-OLCOTT
KATHLEEN A. HINCHMAN

THE GUILFORD PRESS
New York   London

© 2005 The Guilford Press
A Division of Guilford Publications, Inc.
72 Spring Street, New York, NY 10012
www.guilford.com

Printed in the United States of America

This book is printed on acid-free paper.

Last digit is print number: 9 8 7 6 5 4 3 2 1

Library of Congress Cataloging-in-Publication Data

Chandler-Olcott, Kelly, 1970–
    Tutoring adolescent literacy learners: a guide for volunteers / by Kelly Chandler-Olcott,
Kathleen A. Hinchman.
        p. cm.—(Solving problems in the teaching of literacy)
    Includes bibliographical references and index.
    ISBN 1-59385-129-4 (pbk.)
    1. Language arts (Middle school)—United States. 2. Language arts (Secondary)—United
States. 3. Tutors and tutoring—United States. I. Hinchman, Kathleen A. II. Title. III. Series.
    LB1631.C4475 2005
    428.′0071′2—dc22

                                                                    2004018480

*In memory of Dr. Columbus "Ted" Grace
and Dr. Peter B. Mosenthal,
valued colleagues and dear friends*

About the Authors

Kelly Chandler-Olcott, EdD, is Associate Professor in Syracuse University's Reading and Language Arts Center, where she teaches literacy courses and directs English Education programs. A former secondary school English teacher in her home state of Maine, she currently pursues research on adolescent literacy, technology-mediated literacy instruction, and classroom inquiry by teachers. Dr. Chandler-Olcott has been working with community service volunteers since 1991, when she codirected a campuswide program at Harvard College.

Kathleen A. Hinchman, PhD, is Associate Professor and Chair of the Reading and Language Arts Center at Syracuse University. Once a middle school teacher, Dr. Hinchman now teaches undergraduate and graduate classes in childhood, adolescent, and adult literacy. Her research focuses on adolescent literacy and literacy teacher education. She has been working with literacy tutors since 1980, including experience with America Reads, Student Literacy Corps, and Literacy Volunteers of America, as well as with preservice teacher education majors.

Acknowledgments

A book always draws on the wisdom and experience of more than the authors listed on its title page. For this reason, we want to thank the following people who made key contributions to this project:

- Our colleagues in the Reading and Language Arts Center at Syracuse University, for their support of us and their important work in the field of literacy.
- Mary Ann Shaw, Associate to the Chancellor at Syracuse University, for her advocacy related to service learning initiatives campuswide.
- Pamela Kirwin Heintz, director of the Center for Public and Community Service, and the CPCS staff members and students involved with the Syracuse University Literacy Corps, for the model of effective and enthusiastic tutoring they provide.
- Teachers and administrators at Franklin Magnet School for the Performing Arts and Grant Middle School in the Syracuse City School District, for their willingness to host tutoring programs for our preservice education students.
- Students in RED 326-625, *Literacy Across the Curriculum*, for allowing us to use excerpts from their work or providing feedback on the manuscript: Amy Branda, Andrew Brechko, Kacey Bush, Kathy Connors, Nathan Coolidge, Kate Doniger, Stephanie Fox, Susan Kral, Timothy Krueger, Nancy Kwak, Trina Nocerino, Elizabeth Paushter, Jennifer Pearl, Melissa Porter, Julie Schopp, Barbara Schrom, Matthew Vogt, and Hana Zima.
- Chris Jennison and Chris Coughlin at The Guilford Press, for their help in turning a rough table of contents into a finished manuscript.
- Our families, for supporting our work and reminding us why it's important.

Contents

TUTORING ADOLESCENT LITERACY LEARNERS

Introduction

Welcome to *Tutoring Adolescent Literacy Learners: A Guide for Volunteers*. If you're about to begin this book, you're probably also about to embark on an adventure as a tutor of adolescents. We wish you luck in this endeavor and hope that our text, like the best of the travel guides we've used on vacations, will provide you with a detailed sense of what you might encounter on your journey, while leaving plenty of space for you to make your own choices about how to proceed. Just as travel can do, we expect that tutoring will expand your mind, lead to new realizations about yourself, and help you connect with people whose experiences may have been very different from your own.

To extend the travel metaphor, this introductory chapter is meant to provide you with a road map for the pages that follow. Here we outline the format of the book and tell you a little bit about how we envision its use. Before we do that, however, we want to briefly introduce ourselves as authors, so you'll have a sense of whose voices you're hearing as you read. We work closely together as colleagues at Syracuse University. Before becoming professors, we taught English, reading, and social studies to adolescent students. Now we teach college courses in literacy methods to prospective and practicing teachers. Our offices are side by side in the Syracuse Reading and Language Arts Center, making it possible for us to have had many conversations about this book and its progress while standing in our doorframes (and often procrastinating about our other responsibilities).

In addition to extensive work with adolescents and their teachers, we bring a good deal of experience with literacy tutoring to this project. Kelly began recruiting and training tutors when she served as the codirector of House and Neighborhood Development (HAND), Harvard's campuswide community service program for undergraduates. While teaching at Noble High School in Berwick, Maine, she piloted a peer tutoring program that provided support for struggling learners during their study halls. At Syracuse University she proposed, and now teaches, a course on literacy across the curriculum that requires undergraduates in seven different secondary education programs to serve as literacy tutors at an urban middle school.

Kathy set up her first tutoring program as a middle school teacher 25 years ago. She also developed programs in conjunction with a federal Student Literacy Corps grant, the New York State-sponsored Liberty Partnerships Program, a Syracuse University grant to involve undergraduate education majors in tutoring at a local public school, and Syracuse University's America Reads Work–Study Program. She has been involved with program and materials development locally and nationally for Literacy Volunteers of America, and she has written and presented on the impact of such programs. All of these experiences informed our writing of this book and continue to inform our face-to-face work with tutors like you.

The book is organized into three parts. Part I, *Getting Started*, includes four chapters. Chapter 1, "Contexts for Adolescent Literacy," and Chapter 2, "Literacy Processes," are meant to give you some background information about adolescent students and their learning needs as well as develop your understandings of what literacy is and how it develops over time. Chapter 3, "Defining Your Role as Tutor," and Chapter 4, "Assessing Your Tutee's Strengths, Needs, and Interests," will help you think through the complex issues related to being a tutor and provide you with strategies for getting to know your student. They should be of most use to you at the very beginning of your tutoring experience. The five chapters in Part II, *Tutoring*, address the "nuts and bolts" of what tutors do, with an emphasis on planning your sessions (Chapter 5), selecting and evaluating materials to use (Chapter 6), promoting students' comprehension (Chapter 7), supporting their development as writers (Chapter 8), and promoting their word study and fluency (Chapter 9). Each of these chapters should provide you with a number of different strategies you can adopt and adapt for your sessions, depending on your tutee's needs, and we expect that you will revisit them for new ideas or clarification as your tutoring progresses. Part III, *Follow-Up and Reflection*, includes Chapter 10, "Dealing with Common Problems," and Chapter 11, "Reflecting on Your Tutoring Experience." These chapters will help you make your tutoring as rich and productive as possible by considering how to prevent or deal with various challenges and building in regular opportunities to reflect on and refine your work.

We wrote this book with the understanding that it needed to serve two broad categories of readers: (1) students in university courses that have a service learning or community service component, and (2) volunteers working in schools and community-based organizations. We do not anticipate that you have extensive knowledge of methods of literacy instruction—although you may want to develop such expertise after your initial experiences as a literacy tutor! Moreover, we do not expect you to replace the individuals in your program who do possess this expertise. Rather, we expect that you will supplement the work of those with more expertise by providing adolescents in your charge with one-to-one or small-group support that they may not otherwise receive due to the limited resources of many secondary schools.

Depending on your role, you may approach the text differently. If you are reading it as part of a class, your instructor will probably set the pace for your assignments in light of other course content, and he or she will assign you to read other books and articles on teaching, learning, and literacy that will contribute to your understanding of this text as well. You will likely have a chance to discuss all of these materials with other students who are tutoring under similar conditions. If you are a volunteer reading on your own, we suggest making your way through the book in its entirety before you begin tutoring, as a means of getting an overall sense of the experience ahead of you. (If you're pressed for time, you may want to skim Chapters 5–9 before beginning your sessions and revisit them, as needed, over the course of your tutoring.) Your community-based program may provide opportunities to discuss the book's content during a formal orientation or follow-up meetings. If this is not the case, we recommend sharing your thoughts about your reading informally with other tutors at your site, because your insights and questions can help each other. For additional information, you may want to consult some of the other resources on tutoring and literacy that we recommend in Appendix A.

Throughout this book you will notice that we talk a good deal about the role of the "mentor teacher," despite our recognition that tutoring programs come in a wide range of configurations and take place in a number of sites other than schools. Like Wasik (1998) and Roller (1998), we believe that the most effective literacy tutoring programs include the close involvement of a certified teacher, even if they are sponsored by a community-based organization instead of a school. Some programs place tutors in a particular classroom with a teacher, who then selects the students to be tutored and suggests areas of focus for the sessions. In other instances, the teacher involved with the program might be a reading specialist or volunteer coordinator who trains tutors and monitors their work, even if he or she does not interact with them during every session. What is important is that you have someone with special expertise and training to go to for advice, support, and problem solving. We recommend that determining who plays this role in your program be one of your early goals.

Finally, let us say just a few words about some of our other choices as authors. In an effort to be gender-neutral in our language, we deliberately vary our use of *he* and *she* when referring to student tutees throughout the text. We were particularly conscious of doing so in sections of the text in which we talk about challenging behavior or poor skills—issues that are often stereotypically associated with boys but that you may just as easily encounter when working with girls. For convenience and clarity's sake, we usually write in ways that suggest working with only one tutee at a time, though you will notice that we make a strong case for the social and academic benefits of tutoring adolescents in pairs in Chapter 3. If you are tutoring two students simultaneously, we expect you will make the necessary adjustments in your head as you read. Last but not least, we use a good deal of direct address (e.g., "You may find. . . ." or "Your tutee may. . . .") in the rest of this text, just as we have used it in this introduction. Although this kind of informal address is not common in academic textbooks, we felt it was appropriate for a practical guide such as this one and hope it will remind you that our recommendations are rooted in our personal experience as well as our familiarity with scholarship on both literacy and tutoring programs. In keeping with this spirit, we invite you to correspond with us about your reading experience, should you so choose, using the following e-mail addresses: *kahinchm@syr.edu* for Kathy and *kpchandl@syr.edu* for Kelly.

Best wishes for your reading and tutoring!

PART I

GETTING STARTED

CHAPTER 1

Contexts for Adolescent Literacy

I had the girls read a list of nine words taken from the story. They then wrote the words on a sheet of paper under four categories, ranging from "I don't know the meaning" and "I *think* I know a meaning" to "Don't know at all"—an idea that I got from Allen (1999). While taking turns reading, I had them stop and write down any word they were confused about. During reading, I would at times have them look at context to gain an understanding of the word. I used gestures, my own words, and facial expressions to help them, too. They would periodically speak to each other in Bosnian to share ideas and help each other to understand. When we were reading, I went through their list of unknown words—giving my own descriptions—telling them to write words, clues, and pictures next to the words to help them. We worked through the list together, cooperatively. They asked if they could take the lists home to rewrite, developing the definitions. I agreed, and they'll bring them back Monday. Best thing of all: Ana said I was a good teacher. Makes all the difference.

—Literacy tutor Barbara Schrom

Congratulations on your choice to be an adolescent literacy tutor! Like Barbara, a student in secondary education who tutored two adolescent girls from Bosnia, you can make a huge difference in a young person's life: modeling behaviors of a good reader, helping to figure out the meanings of unknown words, and offering a dependable presence. Many teens live in a small circle of friends, family, and teachers. Your presence will introduce an additional literate role model and, as a result, a more varied world. In fact, your service will help the young person who is assigned to you in multiple ways that will matter a good deal, whether you're doing this as a volunteer or to fulfill a course requirement.

Being literate is critical to participation in our society—or, as an administrator friend of ours put it, "non-negotiable"—if one is to be successful in our world. Grade-school children can't develop all the skills and strategies they need to know to become literate adults, no matter how effective their initial instruction is.

Instead, young people need support as they develop the strategies to approach the increasingly complex literacy tasks required by their lives, now and in the future. As Vacca and Alvermann (1998) suggested, "Adolescent literacy development is of critical importance because it helps students to develop strategies by which they can negotiate meaning in and think critically about their life—both in school and outside school" (p. 1). There is little you can do to help an individual that could be more important.

This chapter opens with a discussion of adolescents' perspectives toward literacy and secondary school. It also discusses how secondary schools are structured and how those structures can shape literacy teaching and learning. It considers current trends in adolescent literacy education by reviewing principles of instruction and considering the implications of those principles for tutoring. It invites you to project into the future, considering the multiple literacies that will be required of citizens in a rapidly changing technological society. Finally, it discusses the rationales for, and joys of, tutoring adolescents in such a complex, evolving world.

WHO ARE TODAY'S ADOLESCENTS?

When we recall our lives between, say, the ages of 13 and 19, how many of us would focus on the academic world as the setting for our most important moments? It's true that some of us would tell of a teacher who liked a poem we wrote, an examination on which we received a particularly good grade, or, conversely, a test or class we failed. Probably more of us, however, would tell about life in the school cafeteria, a first crush, an unplanned pregnancy, a best friend, a first experience with alcohol or drugs, a winning goal in a close soccer game, a hobby that dominated our spare time, or our first part-time job. For many of us, academics took their place among other priorities—sometimes even *after* other priorities—as we moved toward adulthood.

The world is even more complex for today's youth. The years between grade 6 and high school graduation require them to deal with very different maturation issues, and individuals deal with those issues in very different ways. Some glue themselves to friendly teachers, coaches, or other youth leaders, spending all their spare time with important adults. Others make a habit of studiously ignoring or even flouting adults, living within a tight circle of influential peers. Some mimic pop culture in dress and talk. Others sample adult pleasure-seeking pursuits. Some read and write voraciously, whereas others have yet to complete the reading of a single book.

As a result, to say that the age group is an exciting and complicated one is an understatement. Full of joy one minute and indignation the next, younger adolescents and older youth vary widely in height, weight, mood, maturity, and group affiliation as they grapple with complex friendships and responsibilities. They are often admonished by adults—parents and teachers—that "Things will be different when you are in the real world." But school shootings, gang violence, suicides, and even college admissions data remind them, and us, that they already live in a world that sends mixed messages about challenge and hope.

Middle school students can be particularly enigmatic. As Julie Schopp, a preservice social studies teacher, observed after her first day at her middle school tutoring placement, youth in this age group can seem to be "a mix of shy and hyper," immersed in what Julie called the "middle school rush." Older youth can seem steadier, but turmoil often lies beneath the surface of their apparent calm, as they struggle with many questions, such as the following, that do not have easy answers:

- "What will I do when I finish high school—that is, *if* I finish high school?"
- "Should I apply to colleges near my boyfriend?"
- "How can I fill out all these applications when I have to go to work as soon as school is out?"
- "Does anyone care about a bench-warming basketball player after high school?"
- "How will I continue my education when I can't afford child care?"

All this is meant to suggest that the world for teenagers is, already, very real and complicated. Such a world leaves them not well served by the term *adolescence*, a label that carries images of pimpled, giggly, hormonally driven pleasure seekers (*Ferris Buehler's Day Off* writ large). This unfair stereotype can reduce individuals' varied struggles to make sense of their worlds to a stage—a stop on the way to an adulthood where what is fuzzy somehow becomes suddenly clear (Lesko, 2000).

Central to our advice to you throughout this text is the recommendation that you need to form a relationship with your tutee, one that will allow you to see beyond the stereotypes related to youth and learn what makes this young person's ways of thinking and being in the world unique and precious. This perspective, in turn, will help you to find ways of teaching that will suit your relationship, beginning with your tutee's particular areas of strength and need.

LITERACY IN AND OUT OF SCHOOL

Many people understand literacy to be something that goes hand in hand with schooling, but we've come to see that as a limited perspective. To be sure, many of us did learn a good deal of what we know about how to read and write in school, but it's important to note that our caretakers often played an important role in this development. Reading and writing are part of a larger skill set that includes all of our language development, including the ability to speak and listen. Moreover, our competence as communicators varies as we find ourselves in settings and using media not typically associated with school. Researcher and former teacher Donna Alvermann (2001) reminds us that there is more to youth's literacy than what is visible in academic settings or tests. In fact, focusing solely on the reading-and-writing tasks associated with formal school subjects can cause students who do not complete those tasks as well as others to feel incapable or even stupid. These same students may well have out-of-school interests that allow them to be quite literate, such as playing video games, participating in sports, or playing Pokemon with friends.

Researchers have discovered much about out-of-school literacy that astute tutors will want to know as they work with young people. For instance, Finders (1997) found that seventh graders had a great interest in reading " 'zines" (e.g., teen magazines), whereas Knobel and Lankshear (2002) found that high school students had an interest in producing them. Moje (2000b) discovered that gang-affiliated young people used graffiti, poetry, and notes to express themselves in ways that helped them to develop a sense of belonging; Lewis and Fabos (1999) learned that youth's instant messaging practices often involved sophisticated ways of writing to different audiences; and Chandler-Olcott and Mahar (2003) found that middle school students' online communication about their interest in anime, or Japanese-style animation, helped them become more skillful as both artists and technology users. All of these studies suggest that it is important to get to know the youth with whom you work, and to discover and celebrate their out-of-school prowess when you can.

You will want to know about such interests as you develop ways of working with your tutee (or tutees), even if the focus of your tutoring sessions is supposed to be on more academic notions of literacy. Indeed, developing a student's own stories, poems, or other personal texts can be quite an effective way of supporting writing development. Youth can develop reading strategies through paired reading and discussion around texts of interest to them. For example, Melissa Porter, a tutor with whom Kelly worked, designed a lesson using poems by contemporary rapper Tupac Shakur and Harlem Renaissance writer Langston Hughes that connected her tutee's interest in rap music to literature he was more likely to read in his English class (see Appendix C for Melissa's plan and postsession reflection for this lesson). The lesson honored her tutee's strengths (he had listened to a lot of hip-hop songs!) at the same time it helped him to practice a reading strategy—the comparison and contrast of two texts—valued highly in schools. As time passes and rapport builds, savvy tutors such as Melissa are often able to find more and more ways to tie interests and skills that young people develop on their own to the kinds of tasks required by school.

This point leads us to another crucial question: What does school look like to today's youth? Despite the new challenges facing young people growing up in an increasingly complex world, the basic structures of middle schools and junior and senior high schools in the United States have not changed much in the last 100 years. Designed to reflect the priorities of the Industrial Age, their multiple periods of subject-area study were developed to educate with efficiency as many individuals as possible in the specific disciplines that were deemed important a century ago.

Over the years since that time, discipline-oriented learning has often devolved into a detail-oriented study of isolated facts. With rare exception, such work has been orchestrated via lecture and whole-class discussion to help students learn the information they need for passing tests and college entrance examinations. Students who do well are typically those who figure out how to turn in homework, write five-paragraph essays, and do well on tests. If much reading is encouraged at all, it is often textbook reading relegated to homework, which then serves as a backup to information shared in class lectures (Goodlad, 1984; Sizer, 1984). Literacy researchers Richard and Joanne Vacca (2002) critique this dominant pattern of instruction as "assign-and-tell," describing the classroom routine with these steps:

> *Assign* a text to read (usually with questions to be answered) for homework; then, in subsequent lessons, *tell* students through question-and-answer routines what the material they read was about, explaining the ideas and information that the students encountered in print. (p. 6)

Although this approach, likely to be familiar to many of us, does aid teachers in "covering" content efficiently, it does not help much to develop students' ability to read and understand a text on their own.

From an adolescent's point of view, such schooling can often feel very alienating. Elizabeth Moje (2000a) shared the story of Khek, a young woman of Laotian descent whose ethnicity, race, social class, and gender made her a minority in the school she attended. Khek felt marginalized, alone, and disconnected from most of her teachers and classmates. She explained how her participation in a Salt Lake City gang gave her a feeling of belonging, saying, "Well, Elizabeth, I guess I just wanted to be part of the story" (p. 1). Such youth gravitate toward contexts within which they feel competent and appreciated, even if they are not the contexts which adults in their school settings might desire for them.

Of course, some youth don't make Khek's choices. Instead, they are torn by competing demands to do "what's right" in a more traditional sense. Kathy met Keisha during a study she conducted with 10th graders in a global studies class. Describing how her life as a busy student involved juggling school, marching band, church, friendships, and family, Keisha confessed to Kathy that it left her with little time to make sense of schoolwork. She said, "I like it when I understand. I just don't always have time" (Hinchman & Zalewski, 1996, p. 91). In most cases, her priorities included completing assignments and passing tests but not developing concepts or refining her literacy skills. She cut compromises related to deeper understanding because she saw that as the best way to be successful, given the organization of school and her own multiple priorities.

Researcher and former secondary teacher William Bintz (1993) surveyed a number of high school students about their literacy practices. He found a few avid readers in his study's sample, but many more passive and reluctant readers—individuals who read mostly for school and who, like Keisha, had difficulty monitoring their comprehension. These youth avoided reading when they could, finding other ways to obtain the required information. Bintz also found that even avid readers understood that their teachers often thought that they did not read—simply because they did not like to read materials assigned in school. The students in this study did not use the same set of reading strategies to complete required school reading as they did for reading completed outside of school—partly because they knew that teachers would tell them the most important information they needed to know in class discussions! In such contexts, they really didn't need to read.

The recent report of the National Assessment of Educational Progress (NAEP) presented national data that is even more worrisome. This group has been sampling reading comprehension at three grade levels regularly since the early 1970s. NAEP data show that reading achievement scores have been rising at the 4th-grade level and holding steady at the 8th-grade level but declining at the 12th-grade level, sadly resulting in a lower scaled score for older youth than was achieved in 1992 (National Center for Educational Statistics, 2003). Clearly, schools must change their approaches if they are to capture older students' interest and promote reading before those students exit school to enter college programs or a workforce that demands ever-increasing levels of literacy.

Individuals like Khek and Keisha struggle to balance all that life has to offer, to fit into a world where others admire and respect them. In quoting their voices directly, we hope to demonstrate that the young people with whom you work may see school and literacy in very different ways than you do now, than you did at their age, or than the designers of NAEP tests might hope they would. As a tutor, it will be important for you to avoid imposing ways of making sense on the young people with whom you work. In later chapters we help you acquire ways of finding out about individuals' interests and skills so that you can view learners who struggle with academics in a different, more positive light. This perspective will enable you to be a more effective tutor.

CURRENT TRENDS IN INSTRUCTION FOR ADOLESCENTS

Many recommendations have been made in recent years about reforming middle schools, junior high schools, and senior high schools in the United States (Fullan, 2001; Sizer, 1992). These recommendations often include the kind of school restructuring that can more easily invite our older youth to use their varied talents for school success. For example, reform efforts often recommend small school populations so that staff members can get to know students well. Such reformers also suggest that teachers work to form positive, nurturing relationships with young people, in which they discover and foster the skills the students have developed outside of school. Many reformers also recommend that students take fewer, longer classes so that they can engage in in-depth study that is meaningful to them. At the middle school level, in particular, reform blueprints favor such approaches as *inquiry-based instruction*, in which students generate questions about their lives and the world that then drive their research and writing, or *interdisciplinary study*, in which teachers of several subjects design instruction on topics (e.g., the environment, the fast-food industry, immigration) that help students make connections between subjects such as social studies, science, and English, as well as between school and real-world problems. Instructional models such as these provide opportunities for young people to bring their talents to bear on their studies and to see school as relevant to both their current and future lives.

A smaller group of reformers has made recommendations from a social justice perspective, suggesting that youths engage in projects that will make a real difference to a community, teaching them the importance of such engagement as they learn academic content and skills (e.g., Bigelow, Christensen, Karp, Miner, & Peterson, 1994). Others recommend the development of youths' critical literacy. These individuals suggest that our literacy instruction extend beyond the traditional domains of decoding, writing, and comprehension to help youths understand how people use texts and discourses to represent some perspectives and not others, and to give power to some groups while limiting the power of others (Luke, 2000).

Those who espouse culturally responsive teaching make recommendations that are related to the preceding, but which also ask educators to focus on students' membership in such cultures and communities as their ethnicity, gender, social class, and language status as the grounding point for their learning. This instruction teaches students about how such memberships shape language and literacy practices, and it allows them to understand better the sophistication of their own culture, even if that culture does not match the notions of culture that have dominated U.S. schools for the past century. Such knowledge, in turn, may help youths make important choices about how much expertise they would like to develop with regard to varied discourses, including what has been called the discourse of power, or the mainstream discourse, dominating schools and other institutions (Delpit, 2003).

Although some attempts have been made to implement the preceding reform recommendations, until quite recently only limited attention has been paid to implementing reform that focuses on adolescents' literacy. Notable exceptions are programs implemented in Chicago (Daniels, Bizar, & Zemelman, 2001), San Diego (Fisher, 2001), Oakland, California (Schoenbach, Greenleaf, Cziko, & Hurwitz, 1999), and Kalispell, Montana (Santa, Havens, & Maycumber, 1996). For the most part, though, school funding at the state and federal levels has increasingly been directed toward providing literacy support to students in grades K–3, making it difficult to implement change of any kind in secondary schools. Most of the existing secondary school reforms have been funded by private donors such as the Gates, Carnegie, and Annenberg Foundations.

In recognition of the lack of attention to the literacy needs of adolescents, the International Reading Association formed the Adolescent Literacy Commission in 1997. One of this commission's first tasks was to sponsor the development of a position statement on adolescent literacy. This research-based statement provided teachers, administrators, and policymakers with a blueprint for increasing literacy opportunities for our youth, including several important principles about what adolescents deserve, as a minimum, in their literacy instruction. Outlined in Figure 1.1, these principles can be used to ground your plans for tutoring. For instance, you can help your tutee gain access to a wide variety of reading material (see Principle 1), starting with those materials that he can and wants to read, and following with systematic exposure to other genres. Having observed this individual in comfortable reading environments, you can then show your tutee how to read these alternative sources, as well as discuss what can be interesting about such sources—an approach grounded in Principles 2 and 4.

Like the best literacy teachers, you can have a discussion with your tutee about your assessment of her skills and strategies, inviting her to honestly consider how these strengths and weaknesses play out in varying contexts. This information, in turn, will tell you which reading and study strategies need to be modeled and practiced so that your tutee learns how to do them. Like Barbara Schrom, the tutor we

1. Adolescents deserve access to a wide variety of reading material that they can and want to read.

2. Adolescents deserve instruction that builds both the skill and desire to read increasingly complex materials.

3. Adolescents deserve assessment that shows them their strengths as well as their needs and that guides their teachers to design instruction that will best help them grow as readers.

4. Adolescents deserve expert teachers who model and provide explicit instruction in reading comprehension and study strategies across the curriculum.

5. Adolescents deserve reading specialists who assist individual students having difficulty learning how to read.

6. Adolescents deserve teachers who understand the complexities of individual adolescent readers, respect their differences, and respond to their characteristics.

7. Adolescents deserve homes, communities, and a nation that will support their efforts to achieve advanced levels of literacy and provide the support necessary for them to succeed.

FIGURE 1.1. Principles from *Adolescent Literacy: A Position Statement*. From Moore, Bean, Birdyshaw, and Rycik (1999). Copyright 1999 by the International Reading Association. Reprinted by permission.

quoted at the beginning of this chapter, you can be viewed as a helpful person who cares and who sees potential in the strengths this individual brings into the tutorial.

You can also discuss how to build bridges to the multiple literacies required for life in a rapidly changing, technologically driven society (Alvermann, 2002). You can teach students to use their strategies to search for and judge information on the Internet, where the plethora of ideas and insights is hard to evaluate (Hinchman, Alvermann, Boyd, Brozo, & Vacca, 2003), as well as show them how to publish their own ideas in electronic environments (Knobel & Lankshear, 2002). You can invite them to teach you about their own technology applications (e.g., Chandler-Olcott & Mahar, 2003; Gee, 2003). All of these approaches will make a difference in students' ability to use literacy to be successful in school as well as in their lives beyond the classroom.

WHY TUTOR ADOLESCENTS IN LITERACY?

Your student is unlikely to be the only one who is benefited by your work together, however. Many tutors find that their service helps *them* in many ways, too. First, tutors get to know themselves better as literate beings, because explaining aspects of literacy to others most effectively begins with thought about their own practices—even as they quickly learn not to generalize from their own strengths and weaknesses to their students. (We'll discuss this issue more thoroughly in the next chapter.) Second, tutors gain expertise in noting the details of others' perspectives and approaches to literacy tasks, including insights into their own ability to listen and observe. Considering literacy, especially academic literacy, from others' perspectives can be especially helpful to those who plan to become teachers. Third, tutors get a chance to feel what it's like to make a difference to another individual. When a tutee begins to bring his homework to the session to ask for help, divulges information about his hobbies, or shares excerpts with you from his private journals, you will begin to realize that you matter to this individual. Finally, you may get the chance to see your tutee gain insight into more effective literacy practices in ways that show in his reading and writing. To know that you have helped an individual gain heightened access to literacy in such a way is one of the most rewarding feelings in the world. Keep that knowledge close to your heart as you plan your work—you don't want to waste any of this precious time together!

In closing, listen to the words of this tutor, who, after a semester of literacy tutoring in a seventh-grade classroom, wrote:

> "What I do notice is how much *I've* been learning through my experiences as a tutor/observer. Even though I'm not sure how effective I've been, I do know that I'm appreciated. I've had times when the students *choose* to work with me [rather than pursue other activities]!"

Your understanding of adolescents, and of the contexts of adolescent literacy, will help you to better appreciate all the interactions you have with your tutee. Good luck in this important work!

CHAPTER 2

Literacy Processes

Often when people plan lessons, they focus on the content as the source of learning and do not look at techniques and processes as a tool for developing learners. Literacy is about the process: how the students are reading, the different activities and sources that can be used to enhance the reading, as well as the notion of talking and writing being as valid a source of literacy as reading. My experience with my tutees has made me realize how important literacy is. In order to promote students' literacy, I think it is a good idea to make them see that literacy is so versatile, and that no matter what path they choose in life, literacy will be a part of it.

—Literacy tutor Kacey Bush

Preservice teacher Kacey Bush included the preceding paragraph in a reflection she wrote about her experiences tutoring two adolescents in literacy for 12 weeks. Both of her students were new immigrants to the United States who were learning a new language. Because they struggled with both literacy and English, they also struggled, in Kacey's words, to "keep up" in their content area classes such as social studies and science. Kacey's recognition that they needed to be taught learning processes, not just particular pieces of information for a specific class, was an important one. It helped her to structure her lessons in ways that would serve her students long after her stint as a tutor had ended.

Just as important, Kacey learned from her tutoring experience, and the course she took while serving as a tutor, that literacy is about more than just reading, and reading is about more than just unlocking the relationship between letters and sounds. For a long time, many people viewed learning to read as synonymous with learning to decode words—an idea that still reigns as conventional wisdom for some people today. (It's possible your tutee may subscribe to this view, which

16

could be one of the barriers to his or her success as a literacy learner, something we'll discuss more in subsequent chapters.)

Fortunately for both teachers and tutors, research grounded in such perspectives as cognitive psychology, linguistics, and sociology has illuminated other facets of the fascinating processes we call reading and writing, suggesting that these endeavors require us to integrate numerous different skills and strategies, many of which have far more to do with what's in the reader's head than what's on the page in front of her (Smith, 1985). The role of decoding and recognizing words is important in reading and therefore not to be overlooked (we'll talk more about this in Chapter 9). At the same time, it is only the tip of the iceberg when literacy proficiency is concerned; it is only one small piece of what tutors such as Kacey Bush—and you—need to know and understand in order to be effective. This point is especially salient when tutors are working with adolescents, because they can often decode words reasonably well but still struggle to understand what they read (Schoenbach et al., 1999).

This chapter outlines some of the processes or strategies used by proficient literacy learners and talks about the need to adjust those strategies to the demands of reading and writing in different disciplines. We introduce a way of thinking about instruction—as a gradual release of responsibility—that will help you guide your tutee in the acquisition and refinement of these processes. We close with some discussion of how you might conceptualize your role as a "strategic" tutor— one who uses her tutoring time efficiently and effectively to promote increased strategy use by her tutee.

WHAT PROFICIENT READERS AND WRITERS DO

Over the years, we have found that the best way for prospective tutors to consider what proficient readers and writers do is to reflect on their own processes in a focused way. To this end, as you read this section we ask you to think about several scenarios related to your own literacy, and we guide you in analyzing those scenarios. You might find it helpful to jot a few notes to yourself as you reflect.

We've chosen to discuss strategies or processes used by proficient readers first, followed by those used by proficient writers. This separation of the two is largely for convenience's sake, because, in reality, reading and writing are interrelated processes (Gavelek, Raphael, Biondo, & Wang, 2000). As you begin to tutor, we predict that you'll see that gains in one area often lead to gains in the other. A student who writes regularly about what she reads, for instance, will usually improve her ability to include details in her writing while simultaneously learning how to make personal connections to her reading. Although we focus most of our attention in this guide on print literacy (i.e., reading and writing), the same inter-relationship is true of other language arts such as listening, speaking, and viewing. Any time you can use one in concert with another—for example, asking your tutee to talk about what she knows about a topic before writing or to listen as you read a text to her—your time will be well spent.

Proficient Readers

Think for a minute about the last difficult text you read. Perhaps it was a textbook chapter for a class you're taking or a newspaper article about the economic recession. It might have been instructions for installing a piece of computer software or a pamphlet about the side effects of a new medication. It doesn't matter what the content of the text was, as long as you can recall finding the reading of it more difficult going than is typical for you, and as long as you did manage to make your way through the text. (A difficult reading experience is more likely to allow you to think about your process than one that was easy for you.)

Once you've chosen an experience on which to focus, think about what you did, exactly, as you read. Did you slow down when you came to confusing parts? Reread particular sections? Underline key words? Take notes? Ask yourself questions? Think about what you knew about the topic from other experiences you'd had? We're guessing that you used at least one of these strategies and possibly more as you worked to comprehend the challenging text. Although it's possible that you did sound out some words, especially if there were unfamiliar multisyllabic terms in the text you chose, we're guessing that the vast majority of your reading energy was devoted to other mental processes. When we do a similar exercise to this one in our university classes, most students report that they could pronounce all the words in their text but that it still presented them challenges as readers.

Numerous studies over the past 25 years or so have demonstrated just how complex comprehension actually is. Among a number of key findings, this body of research suggests that one of the most important characteristics of skilled, experienced readers is that they view reading as an active process, not a passive one. In addition, they typically:

- Adjust their reading rate depending on their purpose for reading and the difficulties they encounter in particular texts (Allington, 1983).
- Make connections between what they're reading and their own lives, other texts, and the world around them (Dole, Duffy, Roehler, & Pearson, 1991).
- Ask themselves questions as they read (Singer & Donlan, 1982).
- Visualize as they read and make inferences, or informed guesses, that go beyond the information stated explicitly in the text (Dole, Duffy, Roehler, & Pearson, 1991).
- Determine what information is most important in a text, given their purpose for reading (Winograd, 1984).
- Use a variety of strategies to determine unknown words they encounter (Beers, 2003).
- Monitor when their understanding breaks down and take steps to repair it (Pearson & Fielding, 1991).

Each of these strategies can and should be taught to adolescent readers if they don't already know how to use them efficiently and flexibly. Each would make a fine focus for a tutoring session (or series of sessions). You will find more information about comprehension, fluency, and word study and how you can develop your tutee's abilities in these areas in Chapters 7 and 9.

Proficient Writers

In ways that are similar and often parallel to the proliferation of interest in comprehension research, numerous studies over the past 25 years have revealed the complex orchestration of strategies associated with composition. People no longer see writing as the simple, linear transcription of speech onto the page; instead, they acknowledge it as a process with multiple components that individuals adjust flexibly as they tackle various writing tasks (Emig, 1971; Flower & Hayes, 1977; Graves, 1983). You can engage in the same mental exercise related to your composing if you think about the last difficult piece of writing you did. Maybe it was a research paper for a class or an essay examination. Maybe it was a letter to a newspaper editor about an issue important to you or a poem you wanted to submit for a contest. Again, think specifically about what you did as you composed. Did you make a rough outline on a scrap of paper or in your head? Talk to someone you trust about the points you wanted to make? Gather background material on the topic? Reread carefully to edit for spelling and grammatical errors? Scratch out some parts and insert others?

Although people do tend to develop their own personal, sometimes idiosyncratic, ways of approaching writing, three decades of research suggest that proficient writers also have a good deal in common with each other. Typically, they:

- Consider the purpose and audience for their writing and make adjustments accordingly (Emig, 1971).
- Draw on a predictable set of strategies, including planning/brainstorming, drafting, revising, editing, and publishing, to pursue their writing (Flower & Hayes, 1977).
- Expend more of their energy on getting ideas on paper, especially at the beginning of a writing task, than they do on surface features such as grammar, spelling, or handwriting (Shaughnessy, 1978).
- "Read like writers," or use specific aspects of others' writing as models for their own work (Smith, 1988).

As was the case with the behaviors associated with proficient reading, familiarity with these strategies is sufficiently important to adolescents' academic success for you to plan tutoring activities around them, if you observe or learn from a teacher that your student struggles with one or more of them. We talk more about how to plan lessons that target these strategies in Chapter 8.

If you're taking a literacy class while tutoring, you may be assigned to read additional texts drawing on the research related to proficient reading and writing. If you're not in a class, you might find it useful to seek out some of this information on your own, possibly by reading some of the resources on adolescent literacy that we recommend in Appendix A. Reflection on your own processes and close observation of your tutee's processes, however, should provide enough data to convince you that reading and writing are complex endeavors—far more complex than simply mastering letters and sounds. This knowledge can go a long way in helping you understand why many students continue to require help from adults, including their teachers, parents, and tutors, as they work to become more proficient literacy learners.

LITERACY ACROSS THE CURRICULUM:
PROFICIENCY IN A PARTICULAR CONTEXT

Although it is true that researchers have identified some generic strategies used by proficient readers and writers across contexts, it is also true that these strategies need to be adjusted and adapted when they are applied in different situations, both in and out of school. One of the ways that tutors can help their students most is to guide them in thinking through what it means to read and write well in a particular discipline—say, for example, mathematics or history. An inability to adjust to these different expectations is often one of the traits distinguishing adolescents who struggle in school from those who achieve academic success.

In fact, it is quite likely that your tutee will be skillful at some literacy tasks and not others, and that the differences may be related, at least in part, to how literacy is defined and used in each of the subjects she takes. For example, she may be successful in an English class when asked to read and write a journal entry on a contemporary novel about friendship, but simultaneously struggle to read a chapter and answer questions about infectious diseases from her health textbook. She may receive excellent grades on her lab reports in chemistry class while simultaneously experiencing frustration when asked to write a comparison–contrast essay about primary source documents in social studies. Some of these differences in performance may be attributed to differences in her teachers' styles, expectations, and relationships with students. Some of them, however, can be traced to her lack of sophisticated understanding of what it means to "do" a particular discipline (Gee, 2001)—that is, what it means to read, write, listen, speak, and behave like scientists, for instance, when she is participating in a science class.

That students often struggle to transfer literacy skills from one context to another is one of the most compelling reasons why we believe that teachers of all disciplines need to attend to reading, writing, and oral language in their instruction. We're not alone in this assumption; many teachers and researchers believe that teachers of math, music, health, and so forth, are the best people to teach adolescents to read and write in those subjects. Content specialists, unlike those teachers of subjects traditionally associated with literacy (e.g., English and reading), understand both the material to be taught and the particular ways of using language that are associated with that discipline, and this dual set of understandings can inform their instruction in powerful ways. Moreover, many educators argue that reading and writing can serve as powerful tools for student learning within particular disciplines, thus increasing the chances that young people will learn new content information at higher levels at the same time they develop more sophisticated literacies suited to these texts and contexts. This stance, often associated with the terms "literacy across the curriculum" or "content literacy," is described more fully in a number of resources for teachers, including Alvermann and Phelps (2002), Duke and Sanchez (2000), Gere (1985), and Vacca and Vacca (2002).

If you are pursuing your literacy tutoring responsibilities as part of a teacher education program, a content literacy perspective may have informed your institution's adoption of this requirement. If you do intend to become a secondary teacher, it is likely that you will learn a good deal from tutoring that will inform the reading and writing demonstrations and activities you embed in your future subject-area teaching. If you are tutoring for other reasons, you may consider content literacy as grist for your tutoring sessions, particularly as you get to know your learner and her relative strengths across the curriculum.

Our emphasis on the key role to be played in literacy development by content specialists is not meant to suggest, however, that those who lack discipline-specific content knowledge have no role to play in helping students learn to master discipline-specific literacy skills and strategies. If you're a tutor with literary expertise, for instance, you can still help your tutee to work through what it might mean to read and write in math, and vice versa. Depending on your tutee's strengths and needs, you may indeed be called upon to assist her with reading and writing tasks in subjects beyond your area of expertise. If this is the case, we suggest that you do the following:

- Reflect on your own experiences as a learner in that discipline, particularly during your adolescence, and think specifically about what kinds of reading and writing were valued in that discipline.
- Talk to others—family members, friends, peers in your tutoring program— who have more expertise in the discipline than you do, about the ways that they read and write.
- If possible, communicate with your tutee's teacher and find out what kinds of reading and writing strategies he or she wants your student to work on that will yield more success in a particular class.
- Share the results of these inquiries with your student, reminding her to use those general strategies associated with proficient reading and writing while simultaneously considering how they might need to be adjusted to meet the demands of a specific subject area.

Tutors who raise these issues increase the likelihood that their students will be able to make connections across the various classes (sometimes as many as eight) they take at one time. At the same time, these conversations can help students recognize the crucial differences in how practitioners in different disciplines communicate and construct knowledge. The instructional model we introduce in the next section should help you think about how to structure these conversations in your sessions with your tutee.

GRADUAL RELEASE OF RESPONSIBILITY

In 1983, researchers P. David Pearson and Margaret Gallagher published an article titled "The Instruction of Reading Comprehension," which has been widely read and cited by reading researchers and teachers. After reviewing research on comprehension, the authors laid out a model of explicit instruction using a diagram representing a "journey from total teacher responsibility" for a task to "total student responsibility" (p. 337). According to Pearson and Gallagher, this transition required the use of several instructional components, including modeling, guided practice, independent use, and application. They argued that guided prac-

tice is the most "critical stage of the model" (p. 338) because it turns over responsibility for the task to students in ways they can manage.

This vision of instruction, which came to be known as "gradual release of
responsibility," has been widely embraced by educators, especially those in the
field of literacy, as a way to organize instruction. When teachers work from this
perspective, they keep students on the edge of what they know how to do and help
them to outgrow their current competencies. The clearest and most accessible
summary of the model for teachers that we know is in Stephanie Harvey and Anne
Goudvis's book *Strategies That Work: Teaching Comprehension to Enhance Understanding* (2000). As part of their explanation, Harvey and Goudvis (p. 13) provide the
following bulleted examples of what each of the four components might look like
in practice, when a more "expert other" (Vygotsky, 1978) works with someone
who is learning a new reading strategy:

Teacher modeling
- The teacher explains the strategy.
- The teacher demonstrates how to apply the strategy successfully.
- The teacher thinks aloud to model the mental processes she uses when she
  reads.

Guided practice
- After explicitly modeling, the teacher gradually gives the students more
  responsibility for task completion.
- The teacher and students practice the strategy together.
- The teacher scaffolds the students' attempts and supports student thinking,
  giving feedback during conferring and classroom discussions.
- Students share their thinking processes with each other during paired read-
  ing and small- and large-group discussions.

Independent practice
- After working with the teacher and with other students, the students try to
  apply the strategy on their own.
- The students receive regular feedback from the teacher and other students.

Application of the strategy in real reading situations
- Students apply a clearly understood strategy to a new genre or format.
- Students demonstrate the effective use of a strategy in more difficult text.

Although Harvey and Goudvis's book is focused mostly on reading comprehension, we believe the same four instructional components apply just as easily to
writing. When students are learning a new composing strategy—for example, how
to use a web or chart to plan a piece of writing—it is beneficial for them to be
exposed to expert modeling, to engage in guided practice, to use the strategy independently while the expert observes, and to apply the strategy in a new situation,
perhaps with a completely different writing task. Nearly anything you might want
to teach a learner can be conceptualized in terms of a gradual release of responsibility; it is not just limited to reading, and the "more expert other" need not be a
teacher in a formal setting.

To emphasize this last point as well as help you to think through the elements of this model further, let's apply it to a familiar situation beyond the classroom: a young child learning how to swim. In this case, the expert, most likely a parent or swim instructor, often initiates the child's learning by holding him and allowing him to splash around in the water. Around the same time, the adult and other proficient swimmers—perhaps siblings or older children at the local pool—demonstrate both the process of swimming and its benefits, thereby creating interest on the learner's part in joining the "club" (Smith, 1988), so to speak, of people who know how to swim (*modeling*). As the child becomes more comfortable in the water, the adult may hold him as he learns to stroke or outfit him with gear such as a kickboard or flotation device, so that he can do some of the things associated with swimming without becoming overwhelmed or frightened (*guided practice*). As the learner grows more competent, the adult's role is reduced. The adult may spend less time in the water with the student, choosing instead to offer occasional feedback on a stroke or a dive position from the side of the pool (*independent practice*). Ultimately, perhaps after the young swimmer has demonstrated his competence in tests associated with formal swim classes, he may be allowed to swim in less supervised places such as a local creek or beach (*application of the strategy/skill in new situations*).

If you compare this example to your potential tutoring, it's easy to make some parallels. One of your crucial jobs as a tutor is to model literacy—both the specific strategies used by proficient readers and writers and the general enthusiasm and enjoyment that proficient learners have for the literacy tasks they choose. You will most certainly want to incorporate guided practice into your sessions—times when you and your tutee share the responsibility for working your way through a reading together or when you actively coach him through a piece of writing. It will also be important for you to provide ample time for your student to read and write on his own, so that you can observe his strategy use and so that he can gain confidence and fluency as a reader and writer. Finally, you will want to structure opportunities for your student to use his newly developed strategies in a different instructional context—one that will allow both of you to assess his learning and ascertain how well he might transfer this learning to a situation beyond your tutoring sessions. Each of these instructional approaches allows you to provide a different level of support to your student as his learning progresses, and each requires you to conceptualize your role as tutor a little differently. We'll provide more concrete details about what this might look like in a literacy-focused lesson in Chapter 5, "Planning Your Tutoring Sessions." In the meantime, however, let us provide some words of encouragement about your ability to use this model, given your status as a new tutor.

LEARNING TO BE A STRATEGIC TUTOR

As you read the material in this last section on how a "more expert other" (Vygotsky, 1978) releases more responsibility to learners over time, you might have been thinking to yourself, "But I'm no literacy expert—how will I do that?" To a certain extent, this is a valid question: as a preservice teacher or volunteer tutor, you aren't likely to have the depth of expertise and knowledge that a trained literacy professional possesses. It is healthy (and advisable!) to recognize the limits of what you know and to seek help from others when you face questions about your tutee that are difficult to answer on the basis of your experience alone.

At the same time, if you have been accepted into a tutoring program as a preservice teacher or volunteer, you have undoubtedly learned to negotiate the literacy demands of a number of different discourse communities. You have devised methods to read and write successfully in academic settings and developed a repertoire of literacy strategies you use in your personal life. These experiences will serve you well as a literacy tutor to adolescents, especially if you reflect on them and learn to use them in your planning and interactions with your student.

Paying Attention to Your Own "Mosaic of Thought"

In a popular book for literacy professionals, Ellin Keene and Susan Zimmermann (1997) argue that reading comprehension should be seen as a "mosaic of thought" because it requires the integration of various strategies to create understanding, just as the impact of a mosaic depends on the integration of many small tiles. In addition to finding this metaphor a useful one for reading, we ascribe to another of these authors' key premises: that adults, including volunteer tutors, can learn how to help students develop more sophisticated literacies by first attending to, and then discussing with others, their own literacy processes. This is one of the key reasons why, at the beginning of this chapter, we asked you to reflect on some reading and writing you've done. We hope that you will continue to observe and think about your own strategy use throughout your tutoring experiences.

At first, this sort of reflection may seem artificial, because most proficient readers and writers don't think consciously about what they do. It's likely that you take your skills and strategies for granted, concentrating far more on the task you want to accomplish than the processes that allow that task to be completed. For the time being, though, it will be helpful for you to attend explicitly to what you do as a literate person, so that you can break those processes down into smaller parts and share them with your student. We suggest keeping track of these processes deliberately, perhaps by jotting down a few notes in a journal or notebook after you engage in some reading or writing tasks that require you to use strategies you could incorporate into your tutoring sessions.

Tutors as "Senior" Readers and Writers

As you plan for the future, it may also be helpful for you to conceptualize your role in your tutee's life as what Zirinsky and Rau (2001) call the "senior reader." In their book *A Classroom of Teenaged Readers*, these authors suggest that it can be productive for teachers to view themselves as "another more experienced reader working with a class of developing young readers" (p. 85), rather than as the "expert" on particular works of literature. According to Zirinsky and Rau, senior readers model their own passion for reading, share their responses to various texts with others, and try to understand how other people read, especially when those approaches are different from their own. Senior readers' most important characteristic, however, is that they "know how to read a difficult text and they are able to share what they know about *how* they read as much as they can share what they know about *what* they've read" (p. 85).

In a tutoring context, you might serve as "senior reader" (or writer, as the phrase fits both kinds of literacy just as easily) if you talk to your student about why a particular author is your favorite or model how you organized your thinking for a thank-you note you wrote. You might demonstrate how you made your way through a challenging text from your own life (e.g., an instructional manual or a textbook from a course you're taking) or show your student how you used an e-mail link on a website to write for more information on a topic of interest. In all of these cases, you'll be helping your student by demonstrating specific literate behaviors, of course, but you'll also be modeling the bigger, and perhaps more important, idea that adults use literacy purposefully in a host of different ways in their lives beyond school.

Conceptualizing your tutoring in terms of being a *senior* reader and writer will help you to recognize the strengths and experiences you bring to your work with adolescents. At the same time, it will help you, and your tutee, to differentiate that role from that of a classroom teacher (a role that you may indeed play one day, but one that is not synonymous with being a successful tutor). We've found, in fact, that many adolescents appreciate it when their tutors present themselves as knowledgeable and helpful but refrain from taking on the authoritarian or hierarchical stance that many students associate with their teachers.

If you are thoughtful about your own reading and writing and willing to share those thoughts honestly with your tutee in the context of a caring relationship (a topic we take up in the next chapter), we are confident that you'll be able to serve as a strategic tutor. As such, you'll promote increased strategy use by your tutee in his reading and writing, and you'll also take advantage of your unique position in his life—as neither teacher nor friend—to serve as a role model and source of support as he builds his skills and knowledge base related to academics and literacy.

CHAPTER 3

Defining Your Role as Tutor

I will not lie—I am intimidated. I keep thinking, unwisely I'm sure, that I better be good at this. Talking with [my mentor teacher] and introducing myself to a classroom of kids put my mind at ease, though. I'm excited about the weeks ahead, even a tad "butterflies in the stomach" excited. I'm confident that I can establish a good relationship with my mentor and my tutee.

—LITERACY TUTOR BARBARA SCHROM

Preservice English teacher Barb Schrom, whom you met in Chapter 1, wrote these words after participating in a tutoring orientation at the site where she was placed as a literacy tutor. Just before her reflection, she had spent about 30 minutes with her mentor teacher, Donnie Nugent, in Mrs. Nugent's English as a Second Language class, but she had yet to meet her tutee individually or to plan a lesson. The first-day feelings she expresses—nervousness, excitement, anticipation—are typical of those experienced by many people before they begin their tutoring in earnest. Like many tutors we've known, Barb sets high expectations for her own work ("I'd better be good at this") and hopes to make a difference for the students with whom she interacts.

When we work with new literacy tutors, we see this swirl of emotions as a healthy sign that individuals are recognizing the importance of the role they are about to play. While we reassure them that they will have plenty of help and support as they tutor, we don't usually say that they shouldn't experience some initial jitters. Walking into someone's life and taking up a portion of her time is something about which you should be concerned in this age when both relationships and time are precious commodities. Whether your tutee is a preteen or a 16-year-old, whether you are tutoring for a class or as a volunteer, you should be prepared to make the time you spend with your student productive and enjoyable for both of you. If you are placed in a middle or high school, you should also plan to learn about the complexities of classroom life by developing a respectful relationship with your mentor teacher—a relationship that may develop in fits and starts throughout your placement, due to that teacher's many other commitments.

This chapter is intended to help you form a mental picture of your tutoring situation to prepare you for the complex nature of what lies ahead. We share some insights about how to establish a positive relationship with your tutee and, if you work in a classroom setting, with your mentor or host teacher. We outline some of your responsibilities to help you prepare for what may arise before you actually begin your sessions. We hope this chapter will also help you begin to understand how important it is to commit your time and energy as fully as you can to this venture.

THE CONTEXT FOR TUTORING

(Most) Everyone Wants Help

The majority of adolescents we've encountered were glad to have help from their tutors, because they recognized that literacy is an area important to their success in school and beyond, and because their literacy struggles have often caused them frustration or embarrassment. Some of the tutors we've trained have received eloquent notes of thanks at the end of their tenure; these communications can often make all the hard work worthwhile. We'll be honest, though: Not all adolescents who struggle with literacy embrace their tutors, especially not at first, nor do they always tell their tutors that they appreciate this help, even when they do. For some students, the arrival of a tutor is a public signal of a weakness that they have often developed elaborate procedures to conceal. For other teens, working with a tutor, regardless of whether it's a university student, a community volunteer, or a peer, violates their sense of what's "cool." If you pull your tutee out of a class to work with him, you might encounter some resistance to missing regularly scheduled classroom activities. You should be prepared for such reactions; do not take them personally. Be persistent: The tutor who maintains a positive attitude, continues to show up every week, and plans literacy activities with real-world implications can almost always break through this kind of resistance. Deep down, whether they show it or not, most adolescents are glad to have someone spend uninterrupted time with them and tailor instruction to their needs and interests.

Similarly, every administrator, classroom teacher, or community center director that we have known appreciates the help of volunteers, particularly in the crucial area of literacy. They know that their resources are overextended, and that, as a result, students can sometimes be lost between the cracks. These individuals welcome the opportunity to have any of their students, especially those about whom they worry the most (Allen, Michalove, & Shockley, 1993), receive special assistance.

You should realize, however, that the context within which this assistance takes place is a complex and busy one. Community center personnel are often overworked and underpaid, juggling multiple responsibilities at the same time. Classroom teachers may have only 30–40 minutes of planning time and 40 minutes of free time during a fast-moving school day (and this often includes lunch!).

The people in your tutoring site will rarely have much time to talk with outsiders, even if these outsiders are helping their students. As a new tutor, please understand this situation and, again, do not take it personally. If you are placed in a classroom, you should spend time watching, helping, and working with the teacher, together figuring out times when you might catch a couple of minutes to confer—even if it means chatting on the telephone or exchanging e-mails. If you are placed in a community center, you may need to be equally creative to find time to talk to program liaisons.

When you go into a setting for the first time, expect that you will disrupt what goes on, and do what you can to minimize the distraction you cause. Remember that students and teachers create expectations for one another's actions from September on, and each classroom has its own chemistry. Try to follow the advice given in Figure 3.1 so that you can fit into the classroom as smoothly as possible. You may want to invite your mentor teachers to review the "Tips for Mentor Teachers Who Work with Tutors" sheet in Appendix D.

If you're tutoring in a nonschool site, you'll need to attend to a different set of concerns. Community centers, even more than schools, are multipurpose organizations. For example, the Dunbar Center in Syracuse—a not-for-profit site for tutors in Syracuse University's Literacy Corps—offers such services as a food pan-

- Be certain to arrange carpools, get directions to the school, and find out where to park before your first day of tutoring. Some tutors even choose to drive the route to the school the day before they tutor, in order to estimate how much time it will take to get there.
- Introduce yourself to the staff at the school or center, including the custodian, the person at the sign-in desk, and the school or center secretary. These people are there to help you, and they will want to make a personal connection to tutors who make regular visits to their building.
- Find out where to sign in and out so that your presence is duly noted. You'll also want to determine the preferred procedure (and phone number) for calling in sick, should you become ill on your tutoring day.
- Wear a name tag, as required by the school or center.
- Find out evacuation procedures and your responsibilities as an adult, should a fire drill or emergency occur.
- Do not ever talk about any students, your mentor teacher, or your center liaison in inappropriate contexts. Use pseudonyms for your tutee(s) if you write about your experiences for a class.
- Do not ever spend time in a room alone with a student.
- Make it clear to your tutee that you are required by law to report anything he or she tells you that suggests he or she might be in danger at home or at school.
- Let your program coordinator know immediately if you see or hear anything that suggests you are unwelcome in your assigned placement.

FIGURE 3.1. Making choices to help you fit the setting.

try, employment assistance, family counseling, and foster-care programs, in addition to academic assistance for children. Tutors who work in such a comprehensive center need to recognize that literacy support and academic intervention are only a small part of the organization's mission. We recommend that individuals who work in these settings become familiar with other offerings and pay attention to how their efforts are connected to and complement other services tutees and their families might receive.

Grade Level Matters

If you're tutoring preteens in an upper elementary setting—say, grade 5 or 6—you may find what is called a self-contained classroom. That is, your mentor teacher spends much of the day with the same group of about 25 students, orchestrating their literacy instruction as well as their subject-area study. This level is the most flexible, because, with the exception of special subjects such as physical education and music, the teacher's schedule may not depend on exact times. This can make it easier for you and your program coordinators to schedule tutoring that will not disrupt your tutee's class participation. Perhaps you can observe and then work with your tutee once or twice each week as other students work in small groups on content similar to your tutoring focus.

If you are placed in a middle or high school, students will probably have to move from class to class according to a precise time schedule. You may be able to tutor during your student's study-hall time. But many schools, particularly those at the middle level, do not have study halls. You will be left to negotiate a schedule for tutoring with classroom teachers who have a set amount of time to meet with their students and who will find it complicated, at best, to break the student away from this work. Do so carefully and with sympathy for the competing concerns teachers have in this age of high-stakes testing, compressed curricula, and tight resources.

Some schools have begun to implement what are called block schedules in order to give students more extended periods of time to engage with course material (Daniels et al., 2001). This means that classes may last for longer than the 40- to 45-minute sessions typical of most traditional secondary schools. You, your mentor teacher, and your tutee will probably not want your tutoring to last for what may be as much as an 80-minute period, so this, too, should be negotiated to allow you to spend a reasonable 30–40 minutes with your tutee. Whenever you decide to schedule your tutoring, make sure, with the help of your mentor teacher or tutoring coordinator, that it interferes as little as possible with implementation of the tutee's regular education plan.

Where to Tutor

Some programs, especially those in community centers, have designated locations for tutoring. Others will squeeze tutors and tutees into spare corners in gymnasiums, cafeterias, and hallways. Some schools require that tutors work with students in a central location, such as a library, where qualified school personnel can supervise them. These expectations vary tremendously, however, so you may find your-self with a choice about where to work with your student.

If you have that choice in a school context, talk to your mentor teacher or pro-gram coordinator about the best place to tutor. There are costs and benefits asso-ciated with both push-in and pull-out tutorials. Sometimes when students are pulled out of their classrooms, especially publicly, they can begin to feel excluded from the community in ways that negatively affect their self-esteem and their treat-ment by other students (Jorgensen, 1998). Push-in tutorials, where you stay in the classroom, cut down on the stigma for students and may allow you and your tutee to work with his or her peers, which can be motivating. At the same time, it may be easier to hear each other and to establish a positive relationship if you leave a busy, noisy classroom. Pull-out tutorials can also be beneficial if students are embarrassed by their poor skills and do not want their peers to see them in the midst of getting extra help. Your student's profile and personal preferences will affect the choices you make.

How the classroom is organized will also affect your decision. Some class-rooms have students coming and going all the time, so that students can leave without much notice. Other classrooms are set up in a workshop style (Atwell, 1998; Rief, 1992) that allows students to make individual choices about reading and writing activities and to pursue those activities at different times; such a struc-ture might allow you to tutor unobtrusively in a corner of the room. Still others have a combination of activities going on and a number of helpers present—a spe-cial education teacher, a speech therapist, an instructional aide—so that your pres-ence will not mean anything exceptional. Talk with others in the site to determine how to minimize any potentially negative impact on your tutee or the class.

There are several other places outside the classroom where tutors can sched-ule productive sessions. Depending on what other events are scheduled there, a library, cafeteria, or even a portion of an auditorium can be productive places to work. There may be resource, tutoring, or study hall rooms available. Libraries and computer rooms offer resources such as magazines, reference books, CD-ROMs, and the Internet, which can be incorporated into your sessions. We like settings where other adults are present, so that you have someone to turn to for help and to protect you and your tutee from the kinds of interactions or accusa-tions that can occur in rare situations. Do check with your tutoring coordinator and the adults present in these settings to assure that your presence fits with how they imagine their space being used.

FORMATS FOR TUTORING

One-to-One

Most people think of tutoring as a one-to-one activity, and there are indeed bene-fits associated with that structure. As Cheatham (1998) points out, one-to-one tutoring allows the tutor to "provide his or her undivided attention to one child, addressing the very specific needs of that one child" (p. 10) in a way that may oth-erwise be difficult. One-to-one tutoring also makes it easier for a tutor to assess a student's progress over time.

Pairs

Tutoring can also occur with pairs of tutees, and we've found this approach can often make it easier to establish rapport with students as well as reduce the number of students in a teacher's classroom who need extra help. Paired tutoring may be particularly appropriate for adolescents, because many teens and preteens thrive on interactions with their peers. For example, when preservice teacher Trina Nocerino's tutee, a middle school boy, seemed disinterested in working with her, Trina reported that she and her mentor, Larry Maxwell, "decided that having another student participate might make the situation more fun for Richard." After Richard's friend Edouardo began coming to tutoring, Trina noted improvement in their sessions:

> "Edouardo is more talkative and quick to respond in discussion. He joined us at the same time we began using the basketball books, and I noticed that Richard expressed his interest through his interactions with his friend. Many of the stories we read required understanding of basketball jargon, and I frequently asked them to clarify terminology to allow them to make connections and realize that using their own knowledge helps them understand and enjoy reading. Richard showed an ability to explain vocabulary and use what he knew about basketball and the culture of schoolyard basketball to make predictions and inferences. Richard and Edouardo shared experiences in dialogue with one another more than talking to me. Edouardo's participation made Richard feel more at ease in the tutoring sessions. Maybe by having a peer to interact with, Richard felt more comfortable opening up and communicating. Edouardo's presence gave Richard a sense of power in the situation."

Likewise, Trina's classmate Barbara Schrom found that it could be helpful to tutor English as a Second Language students as a pair. Both recent refugees to the United States from Bosnia, Barb's tutees were able to rely on each other as resources, using their own language to mediate some of her instruction and profiting from some of the differences in their personalities:

> "Sophia is unafraid to ask me to repeat myself or explain further. Zlata is more hesitant to ask questions, but I prod and ask her questions to get a sense of her understanding. Both girls benefit a lot from talking to each other in their own language in order to get a better sense of vocabulary and concepts."

Paired tutoring in situations like these can provide academic scaffolding for students. It can also reduce the stigma and discomfort attached to conspicuous pull-out tutoring, especially when tutee pairs have a social relationship outside the tutoring sessions.

Small Groups

In our experience, small-group literacy tutoring—sessions with three or more students at a time—is considerably more problematic. Although tutors who are placed in classrooms do often work productively with small groups assigned to complete tasks by their teacher, we have not seen the same success when sessions focused on literacy improvement and intervention include more than two students. First, it is often difficult to find multiple students with similar enough needs that a novice tutor can handle them at once. Second, multiple tutees may be more easily distracted, regardless of whether tutoring occurs inside or outside the classroom; this distractibility may create management problems that a tutor is not equipped to handle. Third, two students can talk with each other and interpret what a tutor is asking them to do in light of their own expectations but remaining focused on the tutor's agenda; in contrast, a larger group of students may be more inclined to stray from that agenda.

Mentor teachers will be best equipped to determine which students can work together effectively in tutoring sessions, although tutees themselves sometimes make suggestions that can be useful. Both Barb Schrom and another student placed in the same school, Amy Branda, ended up working successfully with pairs of tutees when the girls to whom each was assigned asked if they could bring a friend. In both cases, the tutees generally remained focused on their academic work and resisted, with their tutor's help, temptation to socialize too much with their peer.

ESTABLISHING POSITIVE RELATIONSHIPS

Relationships with Mentor Teachers

As we hope we have already made clear, classroom teachers and community-based program coordinators are busy people who may welcome your help but may find it difficult to find extensive amounts of time to talk with you. Their days are filled with teaching, meetings, parent contacts, requests for information, and planning for the next day's activities. They must make compromises about how to use their time with reference to a variety of expectations, including those of their students, students' parents, the school district, and even the state.

It is a good idea for you and your host to find a time to talk before you begin tutoring, perhaps in a meeting before or after school, or by telephone. Construct a tutoring schedule with this individual and stick with it. Explain your understanding of how much time you are supposed to tutor and, perhaps, to observe or work in the classroom, given your program requirements. Ask questions about how your mentor teacher views your students' strengths and needs in literacy, and talk to him or her about goals for developing your tutee's literacy. Negotiate these goals carefully so that they fit your host teacher's objectives for this student, and so that you can plan to address them in a focused, ongoing way throughout the tutoring sessions. Schedule other times at that first meeting so that you and your teacher can talk formally about your progress, at least once or twice more during your time in that placement. It's easier to plan for later meetings before both of your schedules get full.

If part of your time will be spent in your mentor teacher's classroom as an observer, participant, or push-in tutor, discuss his or her expectations for your presence. For example, make sure you're clear about whether your teacher will be comfortable with your moving about the classroom as instruction takes place. Talk

- Ask your mentor teacher to introduce you to students formally. It will be appropriate to explain your purpose for being in the classroom. Ask that students call you Mr. or Ms. Smith or Jones rather than your first name, so that they see you as a professional rather than a peer (unless, of course, you work in a setting where all adults are called by their first names).

- Observe one of your mentor teacher's classes before beginning your tutoring, and continue to observe over the semester or year, if that is possible.

- Ask your mentor teacher for a copy of his or her plans and class handouts on the days when you are there, so that you can follow along and add them to your notes.

- Notice and ask why your host teacher does particular things. Ask especially about use of required texts and curriculum. Ask, too, about the community within which the school is located.

- Systematically observe all students in the class, making notes, over time, about what each seems to be gleaning from classroom activities.

- Make notes about everything you see, but be careful to keep these notes to yourself. We think that it is better to observe and participate when you are in a classroom, and then to make a journal entry at a later, more discreet, time. Do not leave your notes lying around.

- Offer to help your host teacher. Such help might include taking attendance, answering questions for students who are completing seatwork or working in discussion groups, delivering a portion of a lesson, helping with classroom setup, or grading student papers.

FIGURE 3.2. Becoming involved in your mentor teacher's classroom.

about whether you might have the opportunity, with the mentor teacher's guidance, to develop and teach (or even co-teach) a lesson for your tutee's class. We think it would be a good idea to consider the items in Figure 3.2 together, to make sure that you are "on the same page." Good, clear communication up front will prevent confusion for both of you in the future.

Relationships with Tutees

Cathy Roller (1998), the former director of a tutoring program for struggling readers at the University of Iowa, argues that there are two general principles of effective tutoring: (1) establishing a warm, supportive environment, and (2) scaffolding children's learning. We touched briefly on the latter in Chapter 2 when we discussed the gradual release of responsibility model of instruction. We also discuss it in more depth in Chapters 5, 7, 8, and 9. Here, we concentrate on the first of Roller's principles: establishing a warm environment in which learners will be comfortable and able to learn from their mistakes.

In order to establish such an environment, Roller (1998, pp. 57–63) recommends that tutors:

1. *Get to know the learner.* Sessions that are built on your tutee's interests, strengths, and needs are more likely to be engaging than those that are generic.
2. *Give specific praise.* Telling your tutee exactly what she did well will increase

the likelihood that she'll be able to do it again. It will also increase her confidence. For this reason, provide feedback such as "You read that dialogue
with lots of expression," instead of the more generic "Good reading!"

3. *Keep the session moving.* Sessions that drag or focus too long on one activity
   will bore your tutee and make it less likely that he will want to return to
   work with you. (We suggest engaging in one activity for no more than 15–
   20 minutes, something we'll discuss more in Chapter 5.)

4. *Model your own enjoyment of reading and writing.* If you demonstrate your
   engagement with literacy outside of school, you help your tutee to see a
   real-world payoff for improving her skills. You also model healthy reading
   and writing behaviors that your tutee might adopt. (Some of these were
   described in the "Senior Reader" section of Chapter 2.)

In addition to these sound principles, we offer two others meant to address
the differences between tutoring elementary students, such as those enrolled in
Roller's program, and tutoring adolescents. First, recognize that your tutee has a
number of other commitments in addition to tutoring that are important to him.
In addition to juggling six or seven classes, he may be holding down a part-time
job, caring for other family members, and maintaining significant personal relationships with friends. Be aware of, and sensitive to, these multiple commitments,
and be judicious if you choose to assign any work to be completed outside of your
tutoring sessions. (We generally discourage tutors from assigning homework in
addition to what the school asks of their students; young people assigned for
tutoring often struggle to complete the required work—much less extra assignments—outside of class.) Second, be yourself. Don't try to be a peer to your tutee.
Even if you listen to some of the same music or like the same films, there will likely
be significant differences between you and your student. See yourself as a professional, not a pal, and you will make more progress and probably gain more
respect from your tutee.

COORDINATING WITH YOUR TUTEE'S CLASSROOM PROGRAM

According to Barbara Wasik (1998), a developer and researcher of several literacy
tutoring programs:

> Coordination between tutoring and classroom instruction is beneficial to the child. It
> is easier for a child who is struggling with learning to read to receive the same method
> of reading instruction with the same or similar materials in the classroom and during
> tutoring. If the tutor works with the child on some of the same stories that are pre-
> sented in class, the child has repeated opportunities to work on challenging materials.
> An at-risk child has enough trouble learning one approach in reading without having
> to juggle or reconcile two different approaches. (p. 569)

For this reason, we suggest that you gather as much information as possible
about the existing literacy program for your tutee. Even if you're pursuing your
tutoring within a community-based organization, you will still want a sense of what

your student's classroom teachers expect of him. You should certainly examine materials from classes (keeping in mind that they may be too difficult for your student, causing him considerable frustration). You should ask him to explain what is going on in class, because his answers can provide considerable insight on how he perceives both the work he is being asked to do and his own skill levels as a literacy learner. You might also want to call or write a note to his teachers, particularly those who teach reading and English language arts, to gather additional information about what the classroom program looks like and how to support it.

Tutors who understand a particular school's approach to literacy are better equipped to help students from that school. For example, at Grant Middle School, where tutors from one of Kelly's secondary education classes are placed, teachers and administrators have made a commitment to a schoolwide literacy focus that includes participation in the Strategic Thinking and Reading Project (STRP; Riggs & Serafin, 1998). STRP has five areas—prior knowledge, inference, vocabulary, text structure, and metacognition—on which teachers focus across the curriculum in grades 6–8. Because of the school's emphasis, tutors who work at Grant quickly became familiar with the STRP strategies and make a deliberate effort to incorporate that language into their sessions with struggling learners. In this way, their efforts reinforce, rather than distract from, the literacy instruction their tutees were getting in other places.

Requests for Homework Help

Some tutors experience problems when their mentor teachers—or, on occasion, their tutees—expect them to coordinate their session *too* closely with the classroom program. Sometimes, mentor teachers see the presence of a literacy tutor as an opportunity for an adolescent to get caught up on missing homework. If your mentor teacher asks you to work with your student on a particular assignment, do not necessarily consider this request a problem, especially if the homework can be used as a context for literacy instruction.

Tutors who consider the literacy possibilities of homework assignments often help their students learn to be more independent learners. During a session with her sixth-grade tutee, for instance, Julie Schopp turned a worksheet of teacher-made questions about the novel *Island of the Blue Dolphins* into a lesson on question–answer relationships—a term used in literacy education to describe "relationships that exist between the type of question asked, the text, and the reader's prior knowledge" (Vacca & Vacca, 2002, p. 370; see also Raphael, 1984). As this approach suggests, Julie taught her tutee, Ashley, to identify whether the answer to a particular question was likely to be found in her head, in the text, or both. In addition to helping Ashley complete an assignment for her mentor teacher, Julie's lesson developed Ashley's ability to find answers on her own for any set of questions, not just the ones she had been assigned most recently. This example demonstrates how tutors can create personalized lessons for their tutees that support the school's academic agenda. Elicit help from your program coordinator, however, if your mentor teacher pushes for a complete focus on homework help; such a focus can interfere with your ability to help the student improve his or her literacy skills. We'll discuss this issue a bit more in Chapters 6 and 10.

Requests for Test Preparation

The standards and high-stakes assessment movements have raised expectations for student performance in literacy and in content-area subjects. Most teachers are being strongly encouraged to help students to prepare and review for these tests. This preparation includes asking students to complete practice exercises designed to help them become familiar with how the tests work. In some cases, this test preparation looks like what you will learn to see as good literacy instruction, but, in others, it provides very limited interactions among students and narrow expectations that can be frustrating for tutees. Although recent research on high-performing schools (e.g., Langer, 2001) suggests that students actually do better on tests when preparation for them is integrated within a rich, ongoing curriculum, many schools continue to promote isolated practice for tests.

Do encourage your teachers to help you engage in literacy activities that are interesting and purposeful for your students. Help them with test preparation only if the situation is dire and teachers really need your help, and then only with a teacher's close support and supervision. As a literacy tutor with limited experience, you are far less equipped than a certified teacher to deal with the gaps in students' knowledge and skills that would cause school personnel to seek test-related intervention for them; therefore, we think it's best for you to concentrate on helping students learn to read and write a variety of expository and narrative texts, topics we'll take up in more depth in subsequent chapters. Such extra help may indeed help students to perform better on tests, and it will certainly serve their literacy development in the long run. It will also help you to learn how to deal with the influences of testing in ways that are likely to make your long-term involvement in schools more productive.

PROFESSIONAL RESPONSIBILITIES AS A LITERACY TUTOR

Your first, and perhaps most important, responsibility as a literacy tutor is to be at every one of your tutoring sessions on time. Kelly tells the students in her literacy-across-the-curriculum course that she expects them to arrive for their tutoring appointments in a timely fashion—unless they are vomiting or bleeding from the mouth. She's only half kidding! If you must be late for, or absent from, tutoring for an unavoidable legitimate reason (e.g., a family emergency, a religious holiday), be sure to call the school or community center to let someone know you won't be coming in. (Giving this notice is especially important if you are working in a classroom where your mentor teacher might be counting on you to lead an activity with groups of students in addition to your tutee.) If possible, give your tutee and mentor teacher some notice about your upcoming absence, so they can plan alternatives. Plan to make up missed time so that your student will not be shortchanged by your absence. Lateness and absences are not only inconvenient and rude to those in your tutoring context, they also communicate to your tutee that you do not see your work with her as a significant commitment. Avoid sending this message at all cost, because it jeopardizes your ability to develop a trusting relationship with your tutee.

New tutors often ask us about what they should wear to their sessions. We first answer that question by reminding them that every professional experience, whether they plan to teach or not, provides them with a possible contact for a later job recommendation or employment opportunity. We think tutors should present themselves with this possibility in mind. More specifically, we refer them—and you—to the school's or center's handbook, which often spells out a dress code for students and teachers. If there are no written rules, notice how teachers or other professionals in the site dress and make choices accordingly (e.g., jeans, hats, extraordinary body jewelry, and revealing clothes are rarely acceptable). When in doubt, we suggest being more conservative rather than less, even if some people at the school or center dress casually. A well-liked, experienced teacher with a reputation for eccentricity can often get away with attire that would not be tolerated if worn by a new tutor.

Finally, you have a professional responsibility to see yourself as a learner and to respect those who are gracious enough to allow you into their school or community center. We frequently visit other people's classrooms in our capacities as researchers, professional developers, and student-teaching supervisors. We have learned over time to treat those visits as data-gathering opportunities, and we try to keep our evaluation of what we see as minimal as possible. This can be difficult; we sometimes see classroom activities that do not much resemble those we would choose if we were teaching. Nonetheless, we find we learn more from our time in those settings when we work to understand what is going on, rather than trying to devise ways to make activities align with the ideals in our heads.

As you observe and participate in learning activities in your mentor teacher's classroom, you may see many practices that appeal to you—ones you want to file in your head for future use if you are a preservice teacher. You may also see practices that don't seem as sound and sensible to you, ones that may even conflict with the recommendations of your professors or methods textbooks. Our best advice to you in these cases is to reserve judgment as long as you can and to gather as much information as possible about why your teacher makes the decisions he or she makes. We're not saying that "anything goes" in a classroom; there is indeed some consensus in most of the academic disciplines about what kinds of activities are likely to result in increased achievement (Zemelman, Daniels, & Hyde, 1998). These recommendations are general, however, and they look different when implemented in different contexts. Orchestrating a productive classroom is more complex than you can imagine, unless you have tried to do so on your own. Because you are probably new to teaching and certainly new to the context in which you will tutor, it is usually not productive to critique the actions of a teacher or center professional. Instead, treat your time in your tutoring site as a good opportunity to learn about the complexity of teaching and learning from perspectives other than your own.

CHAPTER 4

Assessing Your Tutee's Strengths, Needs, and Interests

I have assessed and evaluated Gabriel in many ways. First and foremost, I have made observations from our time together, and I have based lessons for our sessions around them. Some things I have observed are his actions. He doesn't always say what he wants, but he often will indicate through body language that he wants to do something else. For example, during our lesson on text structure, I mentioned in the beginning that we would be using the Internet later on. Not only did he keep asking, "Weren't we going to use the Internet?" but he kept leaning back and stretching until we got over to the computers. I knew from this that he was not interested in the writing assignment we were doing; therefore, instead of dwelling on the writing, which I still thought was important for us to do, I tried to move through it efficiently and quickly.

—Literacy tutor Hana Zima

Volunteer tutor Hana Zima wrote this passage, an excerpt from a case study report, after tutoring an adolescent boy for a semester. We have chosen to open this chapter on assessment with Hana's insights, because we think they reflect the importance of tutors knowing their adolescent tutees well, on a number of levels. Tutors who pay attention to small details in their data gathering about learners over time are well positioned to use that data to develop responsive tutoring plans.

In this chapter, we introduce you to several assessment tools and strategies that can be used to gather helpful information about students' strengths, needs, goals, and interests. We also describe patterns to look for in tutees' work and conversation to determine appropriate next steps for assisting their performance (Bomer, 1999; Tharp & Gallimore, 1989). Finally, we suggest some concrete ways tutors might open up lines of communication with teachers and parents to gather additional data about students from these people who know them best (Rycik, 1998).

(ALMOST) PAINLESS ASSESSMENT

Many people are intimidated by the idea of assessment. When they hear the word, they think of tests. However, we also *assess* when we listen to our stomach growl and decide it's time for lunch. We *assess* when we walk into a room and decide where to sit after noting who is there and where the chairs are. We *assess* when we pick up a book, read the first two paragraphs, and decide whether or not we want to read it.

Teachers engage in informal assessment hundreds of times each day, and so will you when you tutor. You will watch your tutee's dress, mood, and posture, just as Hana did. You will consider how she reacts to certain texts or to particular kinds of tasks, and note these in your tutoring notebook. These ongoing observations will help you to make decisions about what to do the next time you meet. Recorded regularly and systematically, they will become an invaluable tool for your reflection and decision making, helping you to build a more complete portrait of your tutee than you might if you respond only to the things you can remember. You'll have a rich understanding of what she is like over time, and not from opinions formed too quickly. Moreover, if your recording and reflecting are done in collaboration with your student, you will see important results in the development of your relationship and in her literacy skills.

You may be close in age to your tutee or you may have children who are the same age. In either case, adolescents are often greeted with expectations that stereotype them as "typical teens"—and they hate it. Don't assume that because you were once a teenager (perhaps, even recently so) that you know what any particular young person is about. Just because you liked a certain kind of music or book at your tutee's age doesn't mean she will share your passion. Be careful, too, about presuming that adolescents who are involved in such activities as sports, theater, or chess club, or who are raising an infant, will have a predictable profile.

Instead, assume that students with whom you work have unique identities, interests, and abilities, grown out of who they are, where they come from, and those they've selected as friends. They will choose what they want to reveal and when they want to reveal it—as we all do. Literacy is an important thread in this identity patchwork, woven through various aspects of their lives, hopes, and dreams (Moje, 2000a). Assessment can help you to learn enough about your tutee to help you establish a relationship and choose materials and activities for your tutoring sessions, topics we take up later in this text.

GETTING TO KNOW YOUR TUTEE

Literacy Interview

As you begin your tutoring, it's helpful to know something about your student's hobbies, musical tastes, friendships, sports, family, favorite books, school performance, and career aspirations. It is also important to discover what you can about your tutee's attitudes and understandings about reading, writing, and schoolwork. Do remember that students may find it hard to articulate the reasons for their preferences and attitudes if they haven't thought much about such issues before

(Lipson & Wixson, 1996). So, instead of asking, "How do you do in school?" and hearing "All right, I guess," ask, "What kinds of things happened in your science class today? What kind of homework do you usually have?" Figure 4.1 lists a number of questions you could use in early sessions with your learner to get to know him on a variety of levels. The items in Part I will help you to get acquainted with him as a person, whereas those in Part II will likely elicit his perspectives on a variety of literacy- and school-related topics. Feel free to add questions to either part of the list that you think will yield data that you can use to develop a closer relationship with your tutee and plan lessons that will pique his interest.

It may be useful to develop a written survey incorporating some or all of these questions, but many tutees and tutors prefer to find out about each other conversationally. Your tutee may come to trust you more quickly this way, and it may be easier to find interests in common. Take turns asking each other questions, and

Part I: General Questions

1. What do you most like to do in your spare time? With whom?
2. Do you participate in any extracurricular activities at school or at church? If so, tell me a little about them.
3. What kind of music, movies, and/or television shows do you like? Why?
4. Do you have a part-time job? If so, tell me about that.
5. Tell me a little about your family. With whom do you live? Who's important in your life?
6. What do you see yourself doing in 10 years? What colleges, professions, or life choices attract you the most?

Part II: Literacy- and School-Focused Questions

7. Who's a good reader you know? What makes that person a good reader?
8. When [insert name of good reader here] comes to something he or she doesn't know during reading, what does he or she do?
9. Who's a good writer you know? What makes that person a good writer?
10. When [insert name of good writer here] comes to something he or she has a hard time writing, what does he or she do?
11. What was the last thing you read? A book? 'Zines? *TV Guide*? Labels? Song lyrics? Notes from a friend?
12. What was the last thing you wrote, and to whom? A note to a friend? A paper for a teacher?
13. How do you study for a test? What do you do first? What materials do you use?
14. What kinds of work do you do in science class? How do you manage this work? English class? Social studies class? Mathematics class?
15. How much homework do you get in a day? From whom? When do you finish this homework? Where?

FIGURE 4.1. Interview guide for adolescents. The questions in Part II are adapted from Goodman, Watson, and Burke (1987) and Moore and Hinchman (2002).

Athletic

Musical

Amusing

Nice

Diligent

A good friend

FIGURE 4.2. An acrostic name poem for "Amanda."

view your student's questions to you as windows on how she understands her world in comparison to your own. A compromise position might be to administer a written survey to your student first (possibly as a way to obtain an early sample of her writing) and then to have a conversation about the document, taking notes as you go.

Sometimes it's hard to get young people to open up, but Kathy has known tutors who have developed ingenious ways to trade information. Some tutors invite younger teens to use indelible pens to write adjectives describing themselves and their favorite books and music on inexpensive white T-shirts or caps they can take home from the tutoring session. Others have written acrostic poems together, using their own and their tutee's first names and a dictionary or thesaurus to write descriptive adjectives corresponding to each letter (see Figure 4.2 for a sample poem). Some tutors ask students to bring five favorite things to a session, whereas tutors working with older adolescents may themselves bring in a varied stack of books, magazines, music CDs, and movie DVDs, and invite tutees to select and discuss those that look interesting.

Listening Questions

Michel (1994) reminds us to ask what she calls "listening questions" when we talk with learners. That is, ask few questions and listen carefully to answers without inserting your own words. Compare the interchanges in Figure 4.3: The first tutor asked a question and then, not satisfied with Michael's answer, jumped in and answered it himself. The second tutor asked a question and then waited until she received an answer. She didn't fill in the assumed gaps; instead, she acted like she cared about the student's response to the question.

We must share an important caution, though: Do not push your luck as you elicit information. Talk about topics the teen is willing to discuss, and then move on, remembering that you will learn more as you get to know one another over time. Some adolescents need to develop a long-term relationship before they are willing to say very much. Start each session by asking your tutee how she is doing that day, even asking questions about specific classes if it is appropriate to your work together. Don't spend a lot of your tutoring time discussing personal issues—remember that the learner is coming to you for literacy help and not counseling.

Example 1	Example 2
TUTOR: Michael, what is your favorite subject in school? TUTEE: I don't know. TUTOR: Aw, you must have a favorite. Is it math, or history, or music? TUTEE: I hate school!	TUTOR: Michael, what kinds of things do you have to read in social studies class? TUTEE: I don't know. *(Tutor waits.)* TUTEE: We have a textbook, but we don't get to take it home. Sometimes we read Junior Scholastic. Sometimes we go on the Web, but only to things she bookmarks. *(Tutor waits.)* TUTEE: They bookmark because they don't trust us. *(Tutor says nothing.)* TUTEE: Maybe they bookmark because it would take us too long to find some of this stuff by doing a search.

FIGURE 4.3. Comparison of two interchanges between tutor and tutee.

KEEPING A TUTORING NOTEBOOK

Sensitive assessment depends on your ability to review information from various sources and consider its implications for your tutoring. To facilitate this process, we suggest keeping a binder or notebook that includes your plans as well as observations, artifacts, and reflections for your tutoring sessions. Each of these data sources will offer you a different perspective on your tutee's literacy learning.

Observation Notes

You will most likely take observation notes while working with your student. We suggest that you flesh out these notes soon after the session ends, so that you can remember and record as much detail as possible. Tell the student that it will help the two of you to think about activities that will work best, given his needs and interests, and then be certain that you review such notes with him as a regular part of your tutoring activity. In these anecdotal records (Rhodes & Nathenson-Mejia, 1992), note everything you can remember about what you said and what your tutor said and did in response to your initiations, quoting your tutee's words as often as possible. Try not to make judgments (e.g., "He was bored"). Instead, record what happened in more descriptive terms (e.g., "She slouched in her chair, reading each word with hesitation, yawning and sliding further and further in the chair as she read through the page"). Ask your student what he learned from each activity, and record what he said in response. See Figure 4.4 for a sample set of observation notes.

10/16/02   Alexa and I sat together reading and discussing a section of her social studies book. We looked at the heading "The Underground Railroad" when I asked her what information she thought the section was going to contain. She said, "I know it has something to do with slaves escaping to freedom, mostly at night."

We took turns reading the paragraphs in the section aloud. When it was her turn, she read quietly, hesitating on some words. She mispronounced *clandestine*, saying, "Clan . . . clandes . . . I don't know that word." I said it for her and told her it meant *secret*.

When she got to the end of the section, I said, "What do we do next?" She said, "We look back through the passage to be sure we know what it was about, and we figure out a way to map it." I asked her what she thought the passage was about, and she said, "The underground railroad had secret stations that were actually people's houses where they hid away escaped slaves." I said, "Anything else?" She said, "They went to Canada." I asked, "Who were the conductors?" She said, "People who met the slaves at a spot outside the plantation once they'd escaped." We drew a web to show the main ideas.

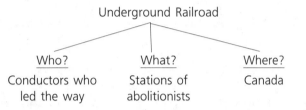

As we were finishing, I asked, "Was the underground railroad a real railroad?" She said, "I don't think so," and we talked about how it was a metaphor for a secret group of people who helped the slaves.

FIGURE 4.4. Sample observation notes.

Artifacts

Include artifacts from tutoring activities in your notebook. These can include such representations of your time together as a running list of texts read, tutee writing samples, student notes, printouts from Internet searches, homework completed for another class, or illustrations of stories. They can also include written or dictated reflections, within which your tutee considers her own strengths and weaknesses in completing a certain reading or writing task. We've even found it useful to have tutors keep a daily tutoring agenda, on which a tutee might record what he learned and liked about each activity (more on this in Chapter 5).

Reflections

Once you've recorded a description of the session and gathered related artifacts, create another entry in your notebook for your reflections about your session. In these, think through all the possible explanations for your tutee's actions (e.g., perhaps she was bored, was up late last night, didn't have breakfast, or didn't like the reading but was being polite). Think of all possible interpretations of the activities you've completed and artifacts you've collected. Tell what you think she

I felt good about what happened today. For the first time, when I asked Nicoletta what she should do when she got to the end of reading the section, she could answer with the idea that she should review and check her understanding of what she read. If she actually does this on her own, she should do a better job reading her homework. But I should have asked her to try to remember to do it when she read between now and our next time together, so she could tell me about it! Oh well, maybe she will remember anyway.

I think that I will try a new prereading strategy the next time we meet. I will have us scan sections of text together and pull out hard words so that I can work out her pronunciation with her before she reads. We can also use this as a preview of the text, so that she can make predictions regarding what the text is going to be about.

I'm going to see if I can find some other reading materials on the Reconstruction period for her to read next time. She seems to find the textbook really boring, and I agree. Library books, even picture books, might let us know in a more in-depth way what life was like during this important time period.

FIGURE 4.5. Sample reflection.

learned from the session. Tell what you learned during the session about your tutee, about tutoring, or about teaching, in general.

We've usually found it helpful to write reflections (a sample is provided in Figure 4.5) so that they can be shared with the tutee. Teenagers are old enough to share their opinions about *your* opinions, and asking for their opinions can tell them that you respect them and their judgment. Considering them to be your first audience will keep your entries from becoming overly critical—a stance, sometimes taken by inexperienced tutors, that can interfere with your relationship with your tutee.

In Chapter 11, we talk more about specific ways you can review your tutoring notebook to reflect on your tutoring experience as a whole. In the meantime, however, we suggest keeping this notebook faithfully and reviewing its contents periodically. Write new reflections from this review, considering changes that have occurred in your relationship with your tutee or in his or her reading or writing, as you consider the trends and themes in your entries over time. These reflections, too, can be done in collaboration with your tutee, especially if the purpose is to discern things your tutee has learned over the course of your time together.

SCHEDULING ASSESSMENTS

It is best not to bombard adolescents with exercises that you call "tests" or "assessments" all at one time—especially at the start of your tutoring relationship. While it's true that you will want to know as much as possible as you begin to work with a student, it is better to cast a wide net with activities that allow the learner to show you what she likes and can do. You'll be able to narrow your understandings of your learner's literacy processes and interests in small bits over time as you continue to tutor.

You will likely receive some assessment results from those who arrange your tutoring match. Some of these assessments will clearly be scientifically based, such as a norm-referenced reading comprehension test whose validity and reliability have been established. Others will be teacher-developed assessments, such as a classroom unit test. All such assessments tell you something about a learner, including, perhaps, how the individual's performance compares to that of peers, or what level of texts the person reads most comfortably.

To teach someone about reading and writing, however, you need to see how the student approaches reading and writing tasks and makes sense of these processes. To do this, you will need to gather some of your own data. You will want to observe your learner read and write, and to ask questions about the strategies used to engage in these processes. Combined with other data that are available, you will begin to develop theories about the individual's literacy that you can check with your learner as the two of you plan a course of action together.

ASSESSING READING COMPREHENSION

Meaning making is the point of reading. Because it is so important, and because you are likely only beginning to understand the other skills that might be needed to help someone develop literacy, comprehension can provide the primary focus for most of your tutoring. Every time you share a text with your tutee and then talk about it, you have a chance to assess comprehension.

Keep in mind that some students do not know that reading is supposed to make sense. Kathy once had a teenage boy tell her that she changed his life because she told him he should "stop and think when you don't understand what you are reading." Others are well able to exercise important sense-making strategies as they read, but have difficulty expressing this understanding orally and/or in writing. Others make sense as they read but are confused by the wording of questions—from teachers, tests, or even tutors. Still other teenagers have difficulties reading expository text but not narrative text. In fact, every time the subject and text type varies, so will your tutee's comfort level, depending on amount and type of previous experience. When you think about it, you likely feel more comfortable reading certain kinds of text than others—although you don't want to let your biases interfere with your attention to the texts with which your student most needs help.

The many factors that affect comprehension are why it is important to gather multiple and varied observations about an individual's comprehension as you tutor. In this way, you can keep refining your hypotheses about what reading means for this student. More important, you should check any tentative conclusions you are drawing with your tutee.

Retellings

One straightforward and informal way to assess comprehension is to ask your tutee to retell what he has just finished reading (Koskinen, Gambrell, Kapinus, & Heathington, 1988; Morrow, 1986). It will help you to draw important inferences about how your student understands and organizes information. To do this, tell your learner before reading that you will be asking him to retell the story or the gist of the text upon completion. Together, pick a passage to use for the exercise that represents a whole story or explanation, and then ask your tutee to read silently. Upon completion, ask him to tell you about what he just read. Encourage him to share everything he remembers, even if it feels a bit awkward (which it probably will, because this is not a usual postreading behavior). During his retelling make notes that preserve his exact language as much as possible.

See Figure 4.6 for an example of a retelling checklist that you might want to use to record and then analyze a retelling. During analysis, consider first whether the passage was narrative or expository, and then how the argument unfolded in the text. If the passage was narrative, see if your tutee included the characters and their feelings, as well as the setting, problem, and solution in the retelling. If the passage was expository, see if the retelling included the main idea and the significant details supporting it. Also, check the retelling to see that the student seemed aware of such features of the text as causes and effects or comparisons and contrasts. Compare retellings your student does across multiple texts, and share these with him. If retellings consistently omit the same components, then they have signaled possible areas for additional instruction.

Assessing Strategy Use Informally

As we discussed in Chapter 2, research suggests that strategic readers exercise particular strategies before, during, and after reading; you will learn to support your tutee's development of these strategies. To decide the focus of your tutoring, you may want to elicit insights about one or more of these strategies. For example, strategic readers preview the text, activate prior knowledge, and set goals before reading. In addition, good readers read selectively, reread, monitor, generate questions, relate text to prior knowledge, develop mental imagery, and determine main ideas during reading. Finally, they reread selectively, summarize, and evaluate text ideas (Pressley, 2002).

Informally, students can be asked to make predictions about the material before reading any text. Make notes about what they say; after a few such occasions, review the notes to identify their nature and focus. You can also check to see if your tutee previews text by flipping through a section or scanning ahead, prior to making predictions, especially if she has been instructed to do so. After reading a descriptive passage, you might ask the student to describe the picture it paints or to talk with you about main ideas or questions raised by it. Finally, you can also ask the tutee to share an oral or written summary or to talk about whether or not she believes an argument in a text and why.

Think Alouds

In addition, you can ask a tutee to think aloud as she reads a short segment of text, stopping at the end of each sentence to tell you how she is solving the problems introduced by the text (Baumann, Jones, & Seifert-Kessell, 1999). This assessment strategy works best if you model such talk for a few minutes—for example: "I know that information in boldface type is usually important, so I'm going to reread

Expository Retelling

Student Name: Date:

Text Title: Text Author:

Text structure elements	Unprompted	Prompted
Main ideas		
Details		
Structure (e.g., main idea–detail, cause–effect, compare–contrast)		

Comments:

Narrative Retelling

Student Name: Date:

Text Title: Text Author:

Story elements	Unprompted	Prompted
Setting (time, place)		
Characters		
Problem		
Events leading to solution		
Solution		

Comments:

FIGURE 4.6. Retelling checklists.

those terms before I go on" or "This part of the text reminds me of a movie I saw about Pearl Harbor, so I'm trying to picture that in my mind as I read."

See what kinds of reading strategies the tutee chooses to share before, during, and after the reading, as well as how she solves problems encountered during the process. What does she do when she comes to a word she doesn't know? What does she do if she doesn't understand the meaning of a sentence? What does she do if she can't figure out what's important in a particular section of text? The answers to all of these questions highlight processes to observe and note for future reference.

ASSESSING ORAL READING

Oral Reading Fluency

Many classroom teachers find it helpful to conduct an "informal reading inventory" (Johnson, Kress, & Pikulski, 1987) as a gauge of a reader's oral reading fluency. Such an assessment also provides some data about word identification ability as well as some signs of comprehension. In an informal reading inventory, a teacher asks a tutee to read aloud progressively more difficult passages. The teacher uses a recording system, such as that found in Figure 4.7, to note the student's oral reading errors, including omissions, substitutions, repetitions, and self-corrections. Some teachers ask students to read passages from classroom reading, and others use published informal reading inventories that contain graded word lists, graded passages for oral reading, and comprehension questions.

Even novice tutors can conduct a simple version of an inventory. Recording oral reading samples over time during tutoring can help you to refine decisions about tutoring focus. To do this, photocopy a text that your learner has selected or is required to read. After marking off a 100-word passage (or a passage of 50

Hesitations	$\overset{H}{\wedge}$ text	Insert a letter *H* when the student pauses or hesitates.
Pronunciation	text $\overset{P}{\wedge}$	Insert a letter *P* when you have to pronounce a word for the student.
Substitutions	text $\overset{test}{\wedge}$	If a student mispronounces a word or substitutes an entirely new word, insert it over the text word that should have been said.
Omissions	(text)	Circle any text the student omits.
Repetitions	<u>text</u>	Underline repetitions, with one line for each.
Self-corrections	$\overset{SC}{\wedge}$ text	Write the letters *SC* for each self-correction.

FIGURE 4.7. Oral reading error marking system.

words or less, if the tutee is struggling a great deal with reading and writing), ask your tutee to predict what the passage will be about from its title and illustrations. Record his response, and then ask him to read the passage aloud. As he does so, record each deviation from the text, using the annotation key found in Figure 4.7. Pronounce words that cause him to stop entirely, and note that you did this. Also make a note when his reading seems word-by-word or choppy, instead of fluent and expressive like talk. Upon completion of the reading, remove the passage from his sight and ask him to retell the passage, making notes about what he says. You should ask questions about main idea, main characters, and significant vocabulary if he does not offer this information in the retelling, and make notes about the answers to your queries.

The data generated during this process can be thought of in two different ways, both of which should be checked with learners and by repeated oral readings. First, let's consider the error pattern. Make a two-column chart. In the right column, print all the words from the text on which the student erred. In the left column, write phonetically exactly what she said. Leave a blank if she omitted a word entirely. Look at this list for patterns (e.g., "missed only words with three or more syllables," "pronounced all words that started with *B* as though they start with *D*," "omitted endings and changed verb tenses"). Then compare your initial guesses about patterns to those portions of the text that the learner read correctly and to other oral reading samples you have collected to check your guesses about whether you, indeed, are seeing a pattern that would benefit from some kind of instructional attention. You will also want to ask yourself if the errors significantly change the meaning of the passage. If they don't, then your tutee may be doing such a great job of reading for meaning that she loses sight of details now and then. This is not likely a big problem and therefore probably not worth attending to in the limited time you have to work with together.

Some readers will reread or self-correct so often that it may seem to disrupt comprehension; this, too, should be noted. Others will read in a word-by-word fashion, suggesting some difficulty in developing some aspect of reading proficiency (Allington, 1983). Elsewhere in this text strategies are shared to help you address this issue.

Oral Reading Accuracy

Another way to think about the oral reading of a passage is tied to long cited research on readability (Betts, 1946/1957), an issue we discuss in Chapter 6. We, like Beers (2003), find the following schema to be a useful way to gauge readability: The research suggests that if the student read the passage with 95–100% accuracy, the passage is easy for the tutee—that is, it is at the tutee's *independent* level. If he read the passage with 90–94% accuracy, then the passage is probably just right to read with a teacher—that is, the passage is at the tutee's *instructional* level. Finally, if he read the passage with less than 90% accuracy, the passage is probably too difficult for him to try without a great deal of support—that is, it is at his *frustration* level. This system gives you a gross estimate; do observe other aspects of your learner's behaviors to determine his actual response to texts at a particular level of difficulty.

If you find yourself sharing a text with a tutee that is at the student's independent level, the confidence the student likely has in this reading means you may want to use this or other similar text as a basis for silent reading and comprehension practice, or you might want to assign it as independent reading. If percentage of miscues indicates that a text is at a student's instructional level, you may want to take turns reading the text, either silently or aloud, to ensure enough fluency for comprehension. Or you might want to consider scaffolding the experience by previewing the text together; providing a mini-lesson on a particular reading strategy, as we recommend in Chapter 7; or helping the tutee to identify and deal with difficult vocabulary, as we recommend in Chapter 9. If the text is frustrating for the student, you may want to select another text for your work together or segment the reading into small-enough chunks that the tutee can be helped to understand it without undue frustration.

ASSESSING WRITING

Composing

Many adolescents are more confident readers than they are writers. All of us who write know how difficult it is to produce a text that communicates well to its intended audience, although those of us with lots of reading experience in our background generally write more easily. Good writers generally follow a predictable pattern that includes some form of planning, drafting, revising, and editing. Some writers use word processors, and some prefer not to or do not have access to such machines.

Depending on how much time you have to spend with your learner, you will want to see how your tutee approaches the variety of writing tasks demanded by the school curriculum. Some of these tasks involve more formal procedural writing—that is, writing produced to explain a procedure of some sort, such as a mathematical solution or science experiment. Essays and reports are another formal type of writing typical to academic settings for adolescents, with variations that depend on subject-area requirements (e.g., data-based questions in social studies, literary comparisons in English language arts classes). Students also take informal notes, keep journals, and write notes to one another.

Think-Alouds

The think-aloud approach can be just as useful in assessing your student's writing as it can be in assessing her reading. Observe your tutee to see how she plans, drafts, revises, and edits various pieces of writing, ranging from journal entries to more formal essays or reports, and make notes about the manner in which she approaches tasks so that you can consider more reflectively how best to help. You may also ask your tutee to think aloud, as we described above for reading, but this time to explain her completion of a writing task. This may be done as the learner is in the process of composing or after the fact. Ask how the planning, drafting, and revising unfolded for her. Ask her to talk you through the composition of each line of a piece of writing.

Writing Samples

It will be important for you to get a sense of how your student organizes and puts words on the page to communicate a point or message to an intended audience. To do this, you can collect school writing samples. You should also collect any writing your tutee does during your tutoring sessions, ranging from informal to formal. You may also want to ask your learner to bring in samples of writing he has completed outside of school, although don't be offended—or get pushy—if the student doesn't think this is a good idea.

What should you look for in these samples? Consider, first, how well the piece communicates the student's ideas to the intended audience. Respond to the content—what you understand and don't understand about the point the learner is trying to make with the piece. Then make a list of communicative strengths and weaknesses, considering which weaknesses may be most easily corrected in light of the strengths (Cheatham, Colvin, & Laminack, 1993). Many students have lots of interesting details to share but have difficulty organizing them into an extended argument that supports a thesis. Others have difficulty understanding the nature of academic writing, thinking that there is some kind of formula by which to organize all pieces of writing. Still other students have difficulty organizing ideas at the paragraph level or coming up with extended ideas for written pieces that are longer than a paragraph.

Just as it can be valuable to share results of comprehension or oral reading assessment with your student to calibrate your interpretations in relation to his ideas, it can also be a good idea to conduct writing-error analysis with your tutee. You may even want to read the piece aloud, so that you and the tutee both hear it and can talk about what it says, compared to what the tutee intended to say. Be sure to identify and discuss both strengths and weaknesses in these conversations, judiciously picking only one or two weaknesses to discuss, which you can then emphasize in your later work together.

Mechanics

Regarding the mechanics of writing, your job is to sleuth out patterns, just as you did with oral reading errors, and decide whether or how to address them instructionally. Adolescents make several common mechanical errors. Many make errors of agreement between subjects and verbs (e.g., "they is") or between adjectives and pronouns and their antecedents (e.g., "child/they"). Other tutees produce sentence fragments (e.g., "I am happy today. Because the sky is blue."), but usually these are the result of punctuation errors and not a dramatic lack of sentence-writing skill, which most students have acquired by the end of first grade. Misspelling of homonyms, such as *there/their/they're* or *to/too/two*, is also a common adolescent writing problem. Occasionally, you will see more significant spelling problems, tied to a limited sight-word vocabulary or to difficulties with understanding patterns in words.

Your tutee's sentence structure and spelling may present both strengths and weaknesses. Don't panic about what you see. If it's possible to do a simple lesson showing him the error pattern and examples of correct usage, then do so, as described in Chapter 9. If you recognize that the student simply does not proof-read his drafts closely enough to find errors, then teach him to read his pieces aloud, even to you, so that he attends to the details of print, and you can ask questions about content. Otherwise, it's better for you to spend most of your tutoring time with limited goals, such as writing in response to reading, planning compositions, or revising and editing existing pieces.

CONSIDERING FORMAL ASSESSMENTS

There are a variety of other tests of decoding, word reading, comprehension, and composition that schools and specialists use to help them identify older students' reading levels. Most require significant amounts of training to administer and interpret. If you are working in a school setting, your tutee's teachers may ask for your help with such work. If so, be certain that you practice administering such assessments before you try to use them with your tutee. In addition, be sure to record results and as many anecdotal notes as you can, so that you and your mentor teacher can interpret the results as accurately as possible.

Be sure that additional assessment tasks are within the purview of your tutoring assignment, as everyone involved sees it. Such tasks need to be useful for your purposes as a volunteer, and to the learner who is participating in such assessments. It may be that your time is better spent actually working on the student's development of a reading strategy.

LISTENING TO OTHERS IN YOUR TUTEE'S LIFE

Teachers' Views

Much assessment of literacy already takes place in U.S. schools. A collaborating classroom teacher might be able to tell you about your tutee's performance on standardized tests or other school or classroom assessments. You may also be able to get access to a reading or resource teacher's more specific assessment results and instructional recommendations.

Remember that tutees might do different things in a one-to-one testing situation than they do in another setting, or with you. For that reason, it's always a good idea to treat every source of data about your tutee with respect—but, at the same time, with some suspicion. If you can get access to data generated by someone else, you'll want to compare and contrast it to what you are able to find out by observation or conversation with your student.

Parents' Expertise

Parents have much experience with watching their children read, write, and do schoolwork, although many parents do not consider this experience as expertise. If you can invite parents to join your collaboration with your student, including helping you to understand your learner's interests, strengths, and weaknesses, you may be even more effective as a tutor. Parents can tell you about earlier school experiences and teacher reports.

However, adolescents are often in the process of trying to gain some independence from their parents, and you should be sensitive to this developmental need. Unless your learner tells you something that seems like it could be harmful to him or others, you will want to keep your learner's confidences. It's probably almost never a good idea to say something to your learner's parents that you haven't worked through with your learner ahead of time. An even better idea is for the two of you to meet with his parents to share progress reports and to ask for additional insights. Parents may also serve as one of the audiences for a case study report, described more fully in Chapter 11.

HOW TO KNOW WHERE TO START

Noting Patterns

By now you have realized that knowing about your learner's literacy means knowing more than a score on a norm-referenced test. Instead, it means getting to know your learner and her point of view. You will listen to her read and talk to her about her writing. You will gather data from teachers and parents. You will look for patterns across data sources to give you a focus for your tutoring. You will pick something you can address efficiently, in the time that is available to you—rather than thinking you are going to solve all of your learner's difficulties. For instance, when a learner tells a tutor about the amount of time she takes completing homework, about how she has to read and reread each assignment, you might ask her to walk through her reading of the textbook, thinking aloud about her comprehension strategies as she turns pages. This might tell you that you need to spend time on how to determine importance in a reading assignment. Because you have a limited amount of time available, you should focus on one content area.

Another learner might be able to read efficiently but have difficulty organizing extensive writing based on reading. He may have special difficulty tying together more than one data source. You will need to help him take notes from the reading and then organize them into a web as a basis for writing. Again, you need to find a way to focus, perhaps tackling the area of how to organize ideas to write in only one or two classes.

Ask the Student

Don't theorize by yourself. Do be sure that you treat all of your interpretations of your tutees' performances as hypotheses to be tested, not as immutable facts. Young people who struggle with reading and writing have thought a lot about what they see others doing, and what they understand they are supposed to be doing themselves. Moreover, reading performance changes, depending on such factors as prior knowledge, motivation, and interest. Writing performance also varies in response to the demands of particular tasks. Furthermore, literacy performance will change as your tutee grows more comfortable in your presence.

Indeed, older students like to hear about what you see as patterns or indicators. You can even ask them about their perception of your gently worded hypotheses. Do share your data and analysis with your learners and tell them about your developing theories. See how your learners respond to your ideas and refine your theories accordingly. Refine them still more after you apply them and find they need more detail to really work within the context of your tutoring relationship.

Set realistic goals that you can address together in the time available. Be sure these goals allow you and your tutee to see progress in small, progressive steps. Instead of becoming paralyzed, thinking you don't know enough to teach, look at your data and think of one area in which you could really help your tutee to learn more efficiently, and organize your tutoring sessions around it.

PART II

TUTORING

CHAPTER 5

Planning Your Tutoring Sessions

The notes in Figure 5.1 came from a literacy tutoring session Amy Branda, one of Kelly's students in English Education, designed and conducted with two sixth graders in an urban middle school. We decided to begin this chapter with Amy's work because we feel it provides a strong yet accessible model of the kind of planning that generally results in successful tutoring sessions with adolescents. Read her plan carefully so that you can analyze it in a number of different ways as you move through the rest of the chapter.

That Amy's tutoring session "went well," to borrow her words, is no accident. She made a thoughtful, deliberate plan for her session, focusing on an important reading strategy (making connections to prior knowledge before and during reading); she built in opportunities for speaking and listening as well as reading and writing; and she included alternatives (e.g., her continuing to read while students made connections) in case her tutees needed extra support. Careful planning does not always ensure that a tutoring session will go well, though. Sometimes, even with the most thorough preparation, a tutor will select a text that is too difficult or choose an activity that a tutee will find tedious or dull. Events beyond a tutor's control—a difficult situation at home, a fight with a friend in the lunchroom—can also interfere with students' ability to concentrate on a lesson. These potential snags aside, however, we think you'll find that time spent planning for your tutoring will reap significant dividends in how smoothly your sessions go and how easily your tutee absorbs new material.

In this chapter we introduce you to important concepts related to literacy lesson planning for adolescents. First, using examples from Amy's lesson plan, we describe a four-component framework for tutoring sessions that draws on the gradual release of responsibility model. (For more examples of this model in action, you can also consult the samples of student lesson plans that appear in Appendix C.) Next, we talk about how tutors can develop a focus for individual tutoring sessions and for their sessions over time. Finally, we discuss how tutors

Tutor: Amy _____ Tutee(s): Alison & Maureen _____

Date: 10/18 _____ Session #: 3 ___

1. Literacy Focus for Lesson (check no more than one or two)

_X_	Making connections	___	Developing fluency
___	Asking questions	___	Considering a model of writing task
___	Visualizing	___	Planning/prewriting
___	Predicting/inferring	___	Organization for writing
___	Dealing with vocabulary	___	Adding supporting details
___	Determining important ideas/summarizing	___	Editing for grammar/spelling

2. Session Goals/Objectives (no more than two or three) *Prior Knowledge/Making Connections*
- *Teach them to cluster (make a web of related ideas) before reading—to brainstorm/make connections to things they already know on topic.*
- *Teach them to make connections to their own experiences as they read.*

3. Texts/Materials
Two nonfiction selections, "Climb-On" and "Ancient Mysteries," from textbook; Post-It notes; and pencil.

4. Procedures for Session Activities
- *Introduction: Define and explain purpose of activating prior knowledge before reading.*
- *Make cluster together of their prior knowledge about climbing that might be useful in reading "Climb-On."*
- *Read first 1½ pages myself and model how to make connections to prior knowledge as I read.*
- *Have them make a cluster of their prior knowledge related to "Ancient Mysteries," another nonfiction selection from the language arts anthology.*
- *Have them read first couple of pages of "Ancient Mysteries" aloud and make connections as I listen and provide feedback (or, if they have trouble, I can read and they can connect).*
- *Have them pick out a book of their choice that looks interesting, then cluster and make connections as they read silently.*
- *Talk together at the end of the session about how making connections before and during reading helped them understand the text.*

5. Plans for Assessing Progress toward Session Goals/Objectives
- *Note the quality of the connections they make to each text.*
- *Save the clusters we make.*
- *Make notes about anything they say regarding making connections when they reflect at the end of the session.*

6. Postsession Reflection
- *The session went well. I was impressed that one of the girls started to make connections right as we began reading. I didn't think they would get it right away, but I think they did. I also felt good when I saw one of the girls underline a word she did not know (remembering the lesson from last week [on dealing with unfamiliar vocabulary]). We ended up reading "Climb-On" the whole time, but I think it would have been better to have switched to the next story. They did start to lose interest after a while.*

FIGURE 5.1. Amy Branda's tutoring plan and reflection.

can keep useful but manageable records about students' progress that will help them in their planning process.

COMPONENTS OF A LITERACY TUTORING SESSION FOR ADOLESCENTS

In Chapter 2, we introduced you to the gradual release of responsibility model of instruction (Pearson & Gallagher, 1983; see also Harvey & Goudvis, 2000). Amy's plan allows us to consider how this model looks in action in a tutoring session and to connect the pieces of her lesson to key trends in adolescent literacy instruction. You probably noticed that her planned sequence of activities began with tutor modeling and explanation—activities in which she provided a good deal of support and scaffolding for her tutees—and ended with the girls' independent practice of the focus strategies in texts they chose. Over the course of the lesson, Amy "released" more of the responsibility for learning to her tutees and provided correspondingly less guidance to them.

This hand-over of responsibility to students was by design, not by chance. Amy planned her session with a framework for tutoring in mind—one that the two of us developed with the help of a steering committee from the school where Amy was placed. We devised such a framework because research and our personal experience suggest that volunteer tutoring programs are most effective when sessions have a consistent structure and when tutors model the use and enjoyment of reading and writing strategies at each session (Clay, 1993; Roller, 1998; Wasik, 1998). Although it is certainly healthy for tutors to innovate on that structure a bit, we've found that the common framework increases quality control for programs as a whole and calms individual tutors' anxieties about their work, especially if they are new to tutoring or inexperienced at a particular grade level. Consequently, we suggest the following sequence for your tutoring sessions that is grounded in the gradual release of responsibility model (please note that our suggested times are approximate and based on a 30- to 40-minute session, which is what we recommend to our own students):

1. *Read-alouds/think-alouds by the tutor focused on one or two reading or writing strategies*—a time when you model and demonstrate, as a more expert reader/writer, some aspect of literacy that will be helpful to your student (see Appendix B for a list of skills and strategies on which to focus) (5–10 minutes).

2. *Guided practice by the tutee of the strategy or strategies*—a time when your student takes over the use of the strategy you've modeled and uses it with your help and participation (10–15 minutes).

3. *Independent reading or writing by the tutee*—a time when your student reads and/or writes a text without your help, often one that he has had a hand in choosing, while you observe and take notes (10–15 minutes).

4. *Oral or written reflection by the tutee on what was learned*—a time when your student either writes to you or talks with you about what she learned, how she might use the skill or strategy in the future, and/or what she still doesn't understand (5 minutes).

Each of these instructional approaches offers different learning possibilities to students and allows tutors to help those students in different ways. A deliberate mix of them increases the chance that your student will internalize new content and strategies from your tutoring sessions. (See adaptations for this framework for your first tutoring session in Figure 5.2.)

Read-Alouds/Think-Alouds

Many people associate teacher (or in this case, tutor) read-alouds with the early grades, mistakenly assuming that they are inappropriate for adolescent learners. We believe the opposite is true, particularly with struggling literacy learners, because these youngsters need to have reading with fluency and expression modeled for them and often need practice in listening comprehension (Allen, 2000). A think-aloud (Baumann et al., 1999) is a variation on a read-aloud and provides additional scaffolding and modeling for learners. During a think-aloud, a teacher or tutor demonstrates an aspect of reading or writing to students while explaining his thinking process as explicitly as possible. Sometimes, the

1. Administer an interest and attitude survey to your tutee, such as the one profiled in Chapter 4. Some tutors like to ask tutees to complete these surveys in writing themselves, because the activity gives the tutor a sample of the student's writing. Others like to interview the student and make notes—an approach that often frees students to provide more information because it requires less work from them!

2. Offer your tutee the chance to ask you a question about yourself for every one that you ask him. One of Kelly's students, Matthew Vogt, tried this approach and found that such mutual disclosure helped him and his tutee create an atmosphere of trust quickly.

3. Ask your tutee to complete a series of stems (e.g., *My favorite class is . . . ; Reading makes me feel . . . ; I wish teachers would . . .*) with a few sentences. Abbreviated writing tasks such as this one can reveal a lot about a learner, and they often seem less intimidating to a struggling writer than a request to write a paragraph, or more, right away.

4. Invite your tutee to read aloud from a selection of favorite texts representing a variety of genres (e.g., fiction, magazine articles, jokebook, etc.). This low-risk reading activity will tell you a lot about your tutee's fluency and reading rate, as well as her preferred genres and topics.

5. Browse the school or public library with your tutee and take note of which books or magazines he selects. Request that the tutee choose at least four or five books that might be interesting to read during your sessions (you can do the same), and ask him to explain his choices to you for additional insight about his preferences.

6. Go online together and ask your tutee to take you to websites she visits regularly (making sure, of course, that they are appropriate for a school context). Pay attention to how she navigates her way around the Internet, and consider using this information to guide future mini-lessons on research strategies.

FIGURE 5.2. Suggested activities for your first day of tutoring.

person thinking aloud will talk about his decision making, in general; other times, he will focus solely on his use of one strategy (e.g., his inferences or his decisions about where to insert more detail in an essay). The former approach is useful in showing learners that most reading and writing tasks require multiple agendas; the latter is probably more common—and perhaps more useful—when working with struggling literacy learners, because it isolates a particular skill or strategy and provides multiple examples of it. According to teacher and author Nancie Atwell (1998), "taking off the top of [her] head" in a think-aloud allows her students access to "the hundreds of choices that I make every time I write" and reveals how she "consider[s] questions of audience, intention, craft, and coherence every step of the way" (p. 332). Although most tutors haven't had nearly as much experience at writing or teaching as Nancie Atwell, as competent readers and writers they make choices and use strategies that can be revealed to learners in their tutoring sessions. Amy, for example, chose to use a think-aloud in her lesson to model how she made personal connections to the story she read with her tutees. You can use a similar approach to model any number of strategies you use with a specific text. Examples of specific think-alouds can be found in Chapters 7, 8, and 9.

Guided Practice

Guided practice is the component of our tutoring framework that promotes the most interaction and collaboration (Cheatham et al., 1993) between tutor and tutee. During this part of the session, tutors invite students to read or write a text and apply what they have learned from the read-aloud or think-aloud. Tutors provide occasional, gentle feedback and assistance as tutees work, particularly if a student asks for it. According to Fountas and Pinnell (2001), guided practice "makes it possible to teach on the cutting edge of students' understanding. Your support is light. You do not take the problem solving away from the student; instead, your teaching helps students read more productively and intensively" (p. 192). When Amy invited her tutees to read the first couple of pages of their textbook selection and use the strategy she modeled, she offered them a chance for guided practice. As she listened to students' reading and to the connections they made, she could assess their understanding of the new content and offer feedback. If necessary, she could reteach the concept or provide additional examples to solidify her tutees' grasp of it. Guided practice in reading and writing provides a crucial bridge between "expert" modeling/explanation and independent literacy activities. It is often the element of instruction that classroom teachers find difficult to orchestrate for large classes of students, so be sure to incorporate plenty of it into your tutoring sessions.

Independent Reading or Writing

A good deal of research evidence suggests that a primary factor distinguishing good readers from poor ones is the amount of time good readers actually spend reading (Allington, 2001; Anderson, Wilson, & Fielding, 1988; Krashen, 1993).

Allington (2001) argues that many approaches to reading remediation and intervention have actually *decreased* struggling learners' reading volume, because they emphasized activities such as the completion of skills worksheets. Similarly, basic writers are often inundated with grammar and usage activities rather than being encouraged to compose fully developed texts of their own (Shaughnessy, 1978). Our tutoring model includes an independent reading/writing component because we believe that struggling literacy learners need *more* time actually reading and writing than their peers, not less. Although modeling and guided practice are key to students' acquisition of new strategies, they need to read and write independently to "own" and refine their understandings. Just as distance runners need to log many miles as they train, so do literacy learners need to read and write—a lot— before they become skilled. For these reasons, Amy's plan built in a chunk of time for students to practice using the connection strategy in a self-selected text. Although her reflection reveals that she ran out of time in this particular session for the self-selected reading (a common problem for new tutors), she did include the component in her plan, and she did promote self-selected reading in other meetings with her tutees—something you will want to do as well. In particular, independent reading and writing can allow you to incorporate texts into your tutoring that your student chooses, which may increase her motivation for, and interest in, literacy.

Oral or Written Reflection

The final component of our tutoring framework is oral or written reflection on what took place during the session. Such reflection is needed to help adolescents develop metacognitive skill—that is, an understanding of their own thinking processes—that will help them to evaluate their use of literacy in and out of school. As Ruth Schoenbach and her colleagues (1999) remind us, "Gaining metacognitive awareness is a necessary step to gaining control of one's mental activity. . . . Moreover, knowledge of one's own thinking is like other kinds of knowledge in that it grows through experience . . . and becomes more automatic with practice" (p. 29). We know from Amy's plans, as well as conversations with her and her tutoring supervisor, that she frequently engaged her two students in informal conversations about their learning. Asking students questions such as "What strategies did you use to figure out what that word meant?" or "How did you figure out what to do next when you got stuck writing that paragraph?" will foster their metacognitive processes, as will having them write a quick paragraph in a learning log about what stood out for them about the lesson. On occasion, tutors and tutees keep dialogue journals, in which the tutee composes a brief entry about the session and the tutor responds with written questions and comments. If both the tutor and the tutee have electronic mail, a dialogue like this could be conducted digitally, allowing for a faster, and possibly more motivating, exchange. However you choose to facilitate reflection in your tutoring session, be sure to communicate with your tutee explicitly about why such reflection will help him or her as a learner—why it isn't just an exercise—and make sure to save time for it at your sessions when things get rushed.

FINDING AND SUSTAINING A FOCUS
FOR YOUR TUTORING SESSIONS

Each of us has had extensive experience helping people to write lesson plans, both in our work with tutors and in our teaching of methods classes. We know that this aspect of tutoring can be one of the most daunting for new tutors, but we have also seen how powerful the writing process can be in helping tutors develop and clarify their thinking. If you are a preservice teacher, planning for tutoring will likely be useful experience for your future career. As Amy Branda wrote, "Writing lesson plans . . . and working in [her mentor teacher's] class is making me start to feel like a teacher more and more."

Here are some tips to help you find and sustain a focus for your tutoring sessions:

Do One or Two Things Well

One of the most common weaknesses of novice tutors' lesson plans is that they try to do too much in a short period of time. Working on one or, at most, two areas of focus is plenty for a 30- to 40-minute session (observant, responsive tutors often realize that many topics require far more time than this—an issue we discuss in more detail later in this chapter). The first thing tutors need to do in their planning is to narrow their focus. Amy's lesson was successful, in no small part, because she focused on just two goals for her tutees' learning: making connections to prior knowledge and asking questions as they read. She could have included a number of other possible goals for the lesson, including the promotion of students' ability to make text-based predictions, to read aloud fluently, or to keep track of their inferences. Wisely, she did not muddy the waters of her session by including all of these possibilities in her plan.

Take a look at this partial list of focus areas from tutors in Kelly's fall 2001 literacy methods class to get a sense of the possibilities for your sessions:

- Using a double-entry journal to keep track of key ideas from reading on one side of the page and make a personal response on the other
- Using a graphic organizer like a web to plan paragraph topics for an essay question
- Determining degree of familiarity (known, acquainted, unknown) with a selection of vocabulary words before reading an assigned article
- Reading a draft of a piece of writing to see where readers might have questions, and adding material to answer those questions
- Previewing chapter titles and section headings to determine what's important in a textbook assignment

As we're sure you noticed as you read through the list, these lesson ideas are high utility: each strategy is central to what proficient readers and writers do, and each can be transferred to a number of different contexts (e.g., students can use a double-entry journal format to help them comprehend their science material as easily as to help them respond to a class novel). At the same time, each strategy is reasonably well defined—something that a tutoring pair could spotlight in a session or series of sessions. (You'll find more ideas about how to focus your lessons in Chapters 7 and 8, as well as in the professional resources we recommend in Appendix A.)

Think about More Than One Session at a Time

Tutors sometimes worry that their students will get bored if they focus on the same strategy or the same text for more than one session. This is usually not the case. Although you will certainly want to think about varying your approaches to keep students engaged and motivated, struggling literacy learners often need repeated opportunities to learn something new, and they will appreciate the chance to practice a strategy in more than one context (e.g., with a text from a different genre or a writing assignment on a different topic). Several lessons that include the same text can allow students to look at that text from different perspectives. Don't be afraid to plan a series of lessons focused on a particular area, such as vocabulary development, revision strategies, or questioning, if conversations with your tutee or your mentor teacher suggest that these are areas of need for your learner. In reflecting on a semester-long experience tutoring Michael, a seventh grader, Hana Zima noted that there had been what she called a "common theme" to her lessons:

> "I was working on building up his strategies, and so I started with prior knowledge. Each lesson I made sure to include it and show many strategies that depend highly on prior knowledge. . . . I believe Michael needs some repetition and more than one way of explaining a topic to fully comprehend it."

As you get to know your tutee, it will be easier for you to develop your own "common themes" for your sessions.

One last word of caution about focus: If you're taking an education class at the same time that you're tutoring, you may be tempted to try out a sampling of all the interesting approaches you learn about on campus. On one level, this is fine: Tutoring practica are usually meant to help preservice teachers make connections between what they read and discuss in class and what happens in the messy, complex world of school. Remember, though, that the needs and interests of your learner should drive the agenda for your tutoring sessions. Most adolescents will benefit more from a series of lessons focused on a few well-chosen strategies than they will from a scattershot approach to tutoring that resembles the topic list of your course syllabus.

PREPARATION FOR TUTORING SESSIONS

Whether you're a community volunteer or a preservice teacher, your tutoring experience will probably give you a new understanding of the time and energy teaching requires. When students who are not education majors take a class from

Kelly that requires a tutoring placement, they often comment about how preparing for a 40-minute tutoring session every week gives them a new appreciation for how many hours secondary teachers spend preparing for a complete day of five or six classes. How much time *you* spend preparing for your tutoring sessions will depend on your experience, the context in which you tutor, and your focus for the lesson. Most teachers spend a great deal of time imagining how a lesson will go before they teach it, whether they write out their plans or not. Similarly, new tutors sometimes spend as many as 3 hours a week in preparation for one 40-minute session. In general, you can expect your preparation time to decrease as you get to know your tutee better and become more experienced at decision making. Do remember, though, that lessons will take longer to prepare if you have to select a text, search the Internet for background information, or create materials for your tutee to use. Although each of these activities can be time consuming, they're worth the investment, because they allow you to "bump up" your personal knowledge of a topic (or of literacy, in general) and to tailor your lesson to your tutee's particular needs.

Some programs require tutors to use a particular form for planning; others provide tutors with choices and allow them to select what feels most comfortable to them. In Appendix B, you'll find a blank copy of the planning and reflection form that Kelly's undergraduate students use for tutoring. If your program does not mandate another form, you may want to use or adapt this one. However you approach preparing for your session, we recommend that you do so formally—on paper and using a standard outline that will remind you to consider such key factors as your long-term goals, your session objectives, and the materials and procedures needed. The simple act of writing down the plan can often be generative, helping tutors to see and avert potential snags in the lesson, estimate the time each component might take, and ensure that all necessary materials are ready before the session begins. Written plans can also be shared with program supervisors or mentor teachers for feedback in ways that a mental plan cannot.

RECORD KEEPING AND ORGANIZATION

Detailed written plans for your session can also aid you in another important aspect of tutoring: record keeping and organization. When you first begin to tutor, you will want to have a system in place for documenting your work with your student, so that you can discuss that work with your tutee's teacher or your program director and so that you and your tutee can consider his growth over time.

We recommend that you obtain a three-ring binder for your tutoring materials. A binder, as opposed to a spiral notebook or a pocket folder, will allow you to file any artifacts from your lessons with your written plans and reflections. It's a good idea to keep clean copies of any texts you photocopy and any materials you create, especially if you're a community volunteer who might "recycle" resources as you work with a number of students over time. You will also want to keep copies, if possible, of your student's written work so you can examine it to determine appropriate next steps and track growth. You might keep a chart taped to the inside cover of your binder that summarizes your sessions (e.g., date, topic, text used) so that you or your tutoring supervisor can review this information at a quick glance. Some tutors choose to write agendas for their sessions (more on this in Figure 5.3) that can be shared, or even collaboratively developed, with tutees; these, too, should be filed in your binder, because they provide a useful record of your work together.

If you haven't typically been the kind of person who keeps an appointment book, you might want to consider doing so—and while we encourage you to keep as regular a tutoring schedule as possible, you'll certainly have to contend with such interruptions as school vacations and teacher conference days. You'll also want to reschedule any tutoring sessions you miss if you have the misfortune to be seriously ill on your tutoring day. Without a date book, it may be difficult for you to remember these changes in your regular tutoring routine.

If you're a preservice teacher taking education courses at the same time you tutor, you will want to develop some strategies to use what you're learning in class in your tutoring. One useful organizational tool might be a pack of colored Post-Its to mark lesson-plan ideas in your reading, so you can return to them easily (e.g., you might designate one color for reading possibilities and another color for writing). Some tutors keep a small notebook in which they jot down ideas for both their tutoring and their future teaching. Systems such as these will help you reduce the time you spend reviewing course materials when you sit down to prepare for a specific session. They will also help you develop organizational skills that will be crucial to your future success as a full-time teacher juggling as many as 150 students in five classes.

In addition to a filing system for your plans and materials, you will need some sort of a scheme for systematically reflecting on your tutoring. In Chapter 4 we discussed the importance of making notes about your impression of the session as soon as possible after it concludes. You will probably be surprised at how much

In the summer clinic Kathy directs for master's students in our literacy education program, tutors develop daily agendas for their sessions that they share with their tutees. Here are some tips for developing and using agendas in your own work with adolescents:

- Write in "kid language" so your tutee will understand your objectives and activities.
- Include enough detail so the agenda helps you and your tutee to stay focused, but not so much that you can't make adjustments as you go, if necessary.
- Ask your tutee to read through the agenda with you before you begin tutoring.
- Leave some elements of the agenda flexible, so that you can elicit students' input. Some tutors like to give students choices in the agenda (e.g., "Jerry will practice asking questions as he reads an article from *Time for Kids* or a piece from *Yahooligans*).
- Take time at the end of the session to review the agenda together, to see how far you got with your plans and to reflect on the relative value of each activity. Include unfinished tasks in the agenda for your next meeting, if you did not complete items that were important.

FIGURE 5.3. Developing an agenda for your tutoring session.

information can be triggered later in your memory by just a few words written on the scene. You might also find it useful to write a few observations about a piece of student work on a Post-It that can be directly attached to the piece itself.

In Chapter 11 we will talk more about how to review a semester or a year's worth of tutoring documentation to consider patterns in your tutee's growth over time. Here we do want to remind you that it can be very helpful to reread your plans, artifacts, and reflections to guide your planning. Tutor Hana Zima often wrote a "quickwrite"—an uncensored, reflective journal entry requiring no more than 5 minutes—to further document her impressions of her sessions with her tutee. As she explains it, rereading these quickwrites every so often provided her with a record of what happened, not just what she planned, and she used that record to help her plan future lessons that built on her previous teaching.

In sum, it is important to plan thoughtfully for each tutoring session, if you and your tutee are to get as much as you can out of your time together. Using a consistent framework ensures that you focus your work on modeling and guiding your tutee's developing reading and writing with concern for gradual release of responsibility. Keeping records about plans and students' responses to sessions will help both tutor and tutee to note progress and to engage in more successful planning.

CHAPTER 6

Selecting and Evaluating Materials for Tutoring

When Trina Nocerino, one of Kelly's undergraduate students, began tutoring at an urban middle school, one of her first goals was to help her tutee, a sixth-grade boy who resisted most school literacy activities, to see reading as fun. Data from informal conversations and a reader's interest survey such as the one described in Chapter 4 revealed Richard's passion for basketball, a sport he played at school and followed at home as a fan of the New York Knicks. Based on this information, Trina scoured several libraries and the Internet to gather basketball-related pieces from different genres, including poetry, biographies, short stories, articles, and website excerpts. From this large pool of possibilities, Trina weeded out those texts that seemed too dated or too difficult for Richard, as well as those that lacked appealing illustrations or design features. In her tutoring sessions, Trina found that Richard was more willing to read books from her final text set, a collection of eight different pieces exploring different aspects of basketball, than he was to read the literature anthology used in his English class. Although he did not become an avid reader in the 13 weeks Trina worked with him, he did demonstrate more engagement with books, especially when he could discuss them with a friend who joined him for tutoring.

We begin this chapter with Richard and Trina's story because we think it illustrates the important role of text selection and evaluation in successful literacy tutoring with adolescents. If you want to help adolescents learn to read and write better, the first step is to choose materials that will interest them and that represent an appropriate level of difficulty. The purpose of this chapter is to provide you with tips and strategies to do just that.

ACCESS TO TEXTS ADOLESCENTS CAN, AND WANT TO, READ

At the center of the International Reading Association's *Adolescent Literacy Position Statement* (Moore et al., 1999), discussed in Chapter 1, are seven principles for supporting adolescents' literacy growth. The first of these principles—and the one on which all of the rest depend—is the following: "Adolescents deserve access to a wide variety of reading material that they can and want to read." We think the verb choices in this sentence are important: adolescents, regardless of their skill level, need texts accessible enough that they *can* read them and interesting enough so that they will *want* to do so.

In our experience, tutoring sessions offer a unique opportunity to make this range of appropriate and engaging reading material available to adolescents. Because literacy tutors are usually not bound by a prescribed curriculum, they often have more latitude around text and topic selection than classroom teachers do, and this flexibility allows them to tailor tutoring sessions to individual learners' needs and interests. When tutors choose texts for—and, just as important, *with*—the individual students they serve, those students develop more confidence as readers and begin to construct a sense of their own reading identities beyond school.

That tutors get to choose texts for their tutees can sometimes be dangerous, though. Some tutors, especially new ones, think it's their job to help students slog through difficult texts one word at a time. This is not true. Although tutoring can provide occasional extra support for adolescents to tackle a challenging text, the bulk of your sessions should be spent interacting with texts that are relatively easy for your tutee to navigate. Don't underestimate the importance of simply providing time, space, and materials for focused independent reading. As literacy professor Richard Allington (2001) reminds us, "Virtually any reading intervention that reliably increases time engaged in reading should be expected to lead to achievement gains" (p. 34).

In addition to your overall goal of increasing your tutee's engagement with literacy by selecting texts on topics of interest, other goals for your sessions will influence your selection of materials. You might choose a text for one or more of the following reasons:

- It is on a topic connected to the curriculum in one or more of your tutee's classes, but it also explores an angle of interest to your tutee (e.g., selections from Stille's nonfiction book *Extraordinary Women Scientists* for the tutee who feels that women's contributions have been left out of her chemistry textbook).
- It lends itself to a strategy lesson (e.g., it requires readers to draw several not-so-obvious conclusions for themselves, allowing a tutor to model how to make an inference).
- It models some aspect of writing (e.g., an engaging beginning or good supporting details for an argument) that you want to discuss with your tutee.

All of these are valid reasons for selecting a particular text to use in your tutoring. We suggest, however, that you keep your tutee's preferences front and center, even when you're trying to meet instructional goals. It won't do you much good to bring in an essay from the *New Yorker* that has terrific supporting details if your tutee finds the topic unappealing or the language difficult to understand.

So, What Do Adolescents Like to Read?

Several recent studies suggest patterns in adolescents' reading preferences. Young people frequently list magazines, scary stories, comics/cartoons, mysteries, adventure stories, joke books, and sports-related books among their favorite reading material (Ivey & Broaddus, 2001; Worthy, Moorman, & Turner, 1999). As you probably noticed, this list includes texts very different from what adolescents are typically asked to read in school—a trend that many educators see as a problem. Because of their flexibility, tutoring sessions may be one of the ways to address what one research team called "the ever-increasing gap between student preferences and materials that schools provide and recommend" (Worthy et al., 1999, p. 23). Figure 6.1 lists a sampling of texts that have recently been "hot" among adolescents we know and that are relatively easy for them to read on their own, or with a little assistance from a tutor.

In addition to these genres cited by Worthy and her colleagues, we have found that adolescents often like to read nonfiction, particularly when they realize that there are attractive and well-written titles on such diverse topics as zoos, forensic detective work, rap music, firefighting, and even the history of personal hygiene (Penny Colman's *Toilets, Bathtubs, Sinks, and Sewers: A History of the Bathroom* [1995b] was a favorite among Kelly's 10th graders). A good source of interesting fact-driven books is the list of winners of the Orbis Pictus Award (*www.ncte.org/elem/pictus*), given annually by the National Council of Teachers of English to promote and recognize excellence in nonfiction for young people. In addition to piquing adolescents' interest in reading, the books on this list will also build your tutees' vocabulary and knowledge of the world, plus model nonfiction

---

The books in the Harry Potter series, by J. K. Rowling

Esperanza Rising, by Pam Munoz Ryan

Jet magazine

Into Thin Air, by Jon Krakauer

www.lyrics.com

Monster, by Walter Dean Myers

Rookie: Tamika Whitmore's First Year in the WNBA, by Joan Anderson

The Sisterhood of the Traveling Pants, by Ann Brashares

Through My Eyes, by Ruby Bridges

The "Trading Spaces" website (*tlc.discovery.com/fansites/tradingspaces/tradingspaces.html*)

You Hear Me: Poems and Writings by Teenage Boys, by Betsy Franco

YM magazine

FIGURE 6.1. Recent "hot" titles among adolescents.

writing styles that are more interesting than the encyclopedia or their content-area textbooks.

Remember as you make selections for tutoring, however, that the trends and patterns we present here were identified through surveys of, or conversations with, *groups* of young people. An individual adolescent may or may not find scary stories or nonfiction picture books appealing, so it will be up to you, as the tutor, to figure out what will work for your tutee. We suggest keeping a running list of all the texts you read together, noting the title, topic, genre, and your tutee's response (e.g., how much she liked it, how difficult it seemed to be). This documentation will help you get a sense of what works best for your tutee, as well as remind you to vary the types of texts you try.

To help you think about matching texts and tutee needs more concretely, Figure 6.2 presents brief profiles of three students of different ages: a sixth grader, an eighth grader, and a high school junior. Their needs as literacy learners differ as well, and each represents a "type" of student we have repeatedly encountered in our work in middle and high schools. For each student, you will find half a dozen text recommendations that might appeal to that young person, given his or her interests, as well as offer opportunities for instruction targeted at their needs as readers and writers. We have organized the lists of suggested materials with those texts we would expect to be least difficult presented first, followed by those we would expect to be more difficult. This sequencing should be seen as a rough guide only, because some of the most reliable indicators of text difficulty, which we discuss later in this chapter, require interaction with the students themselves.

The Importance of Short Texts

You will notice, as you read through our list of suggested possibilities in Figure 6.2, that many of the texts are brief. We firmly believe that frequent work with short texts is one of the best ways to increase the likelihood of success in your tutoring sessions. Authors Stephanie Harvey and Anne Goudvis (2000, pp. 43–44) agree with us, arguing that short texts—picture books, magazine and newspaper articles, poems, and so forth—are most effective for teaching such concepts as comprehension because they are:

- Focused on issues of critical importance to readers of all ages;
- Well crafted, with vivid language and striking illustrations or photographs;
- Self-contained, providing a complete set of thoughts, ideas, and information for learners to mull over;
- Easily reread to clarify confusion and better construct meaning; and
- Authentic, preparing students for the reading they will encounter outside of school (where it is estimated that adults read short texts 80% of the time).

Although all of these points about the value of short texts are relevant to literacy tutoring, several of them are particularly important. First, the self-contained nature of short texts is ideal for tutoring schedules, which rarely allow tutors to see students more than twice a week. If several days—perhaps as many as seven— pass between one of your lessons and the next, it can be difficult for you or your

Student/interests	Excerpts from literacy profile	Primary goal(s) for tutoring	Possible texts for tutoring
Charlie* Grade: 6 Interests and activities: sports, playing tuba and trumpet in band (*Adapted from a case study in Worthy, Broaddus, & Ivey, 2001)	• Reads very slowly, often haltingly, even in materials leveled for second graders • Needs to expand his vocabulary for both reading and writing • Reports that he enjoys reading and writing, even though he struggles with them	• Help him to develop greater reading fluency and confidence (see Chapter 9 for more on this) • Help him to write informally about what he reads so that he understands it better (see Chapter 8 for more on this) and increase his vocabulary knowledge	• *Eyewitness: Music*, by Neil Ardley (nonfiction picture book) • *Charlie Parker Played BeBop*, by Chris Raschka (picture book) • *Hoops* by Robert Burleigh and *Sports Pages* by Arnold Adoff (poetry) • *Ben's Trumpet*, by Rachel Isadora (picture book) • *Teammates*, by Peter Golenbock (picture book biography) • Selected articles from *Sports Illustrated for Kids* (magazine)
Yasmin Grade: 9 Interests and activities: dance, fitness and nutrition, taking care of younger siblings after school	• Decodes fairly well, although she struggles with multisyllabic words • Reads realistic novels avidly, especially those in series, such as the *Gossip Girl* books by Cecily von Ziegesar • Struggles with school reading, particularly with determining what's important in chapters from her science textbook	• Help her learn to determine important material (see Chapter 7 for more on this) in nonfiction text related to science topics as well as her own interests	• *Tallchief*, by Maria Tallchief and Rosemary Wells (picture book biography) • *A Drop of Water*, by Walter Wick (nonfiction picture book) • *The Water Cycle*, by Theresa Greenaway (nonfiction picture book) • Features on women's health and fitness linked to Yahoo's page on Health at *http://health.yahoo.com* (website) • Article from *Time* on low-carbohydrate diets (magazine) • Excerpts from *Fast Food Nation*, by Eric Schlosser (nonfiction)
Jonah Grade: 11 Interests and activities: hiking, hunting, fishing	• Reads really fast, without much expression, but "gets" nearly all of the words right • When he does make oral reading mistakes, they usually don't make much sense, but this doesn't seem to bother him • Tries to get both his reading and writing done as quickly as possibly and says he "never" reads unless he has to	• Help him learn to select reading materials he will enjoy • Teach him to read more actively and strategically, using such strategies as text-to-self connections and questioning (see Chapter 7 for more on this)	• *The Top of the World: Climbing Mount Everest*, by Steve Jenkins (nonfiction picture book) • Excerpts from *Tom Brown's Field Guide to Nature Observation and Tracking*, by Tom Brown (nonfiction) • Chapter 1 from *Winterdance: The Fine Madness of Running the Iditarod*, by Gary Paulsen (memoir) • Articles from *Outside Magazine Online* at *http://outside.away.com/index.html*) (website) • Essay on coyote management in Maine from *Best American Science and Nature Writing, 2003*, edited by Richard Dawkins (nonfiction)

FIGURE 6.2. Text selection possibilities for three adolescents.

tutee to recall exactly where you were in a text you didn't complete. You may waste valuable reading and writing time just trying to recall material that was already covered. Second, the use of short texts also reduces the consequences of making poor choices for your tutee. If you plan your lesson around a four-page essay that turns out to be too hard for your tutee, you can work through the text in one session and make a better choice next time. In contrast, if you choose a lengthy novel to read with your tutee and she decides she hates it after 50 pages, you've invested considerable time and energy in a text you won't bring to any sort of closure (unless—and we don't recommend this—you insist on dragging your tutee through the rest of the book). Even if she doesn't hate it, you may not want that one text to be the basis of your entire tutoring relationship.

Please remember, however, that our advocacy of short texts is a suggestion, not a dictate. If your mentor teacher suggests that you plan some lessons around the novel the class is currently reading, you can certainly agree. If your tutee chooses a longer text as one she wants to work on during some of your sessions, you may want to build on that interest.

SO, HOW DO YOU FIND THESE ENGAGING TEXTS, SHORT OR OTHERWISE?

Once you get to know your tutee, texts for potential tutoring sessions may appear when you're least expecting them. One tutor we know found that numerous new resources on the Holocaust began to cross his path once he had identified that topic as an area of interest for his tutee. Serendipitous discoveries notwithstanding, you will want some deliberate strategies for finding texts suitable for tutoring. Here are some suggestions that should help you:

1. Subscribe to your local newspaper, if you don't already, and start a clippings file of teen-friendly articles.
2. Ask the library media specialist at your school or the youth services coordinator in your community library to recommend picture books, both fiction and nonfiction, that would be appropriate for older readers. If you are looking for titles on a particular topic, these professionals may be able to supplement their collection with titles borrowed from other libraries in the system.
3. While you're at the library, ask the librarian to show you the numerous high-quality magazines published specifically for young people, including *Teen People*, *Sports Illustrated for Kids*, *National Geographic World*, and *Nickelodeon*.
4. If you travel, keep copies of in-flight magazines such as Delta's *Sky Magazine*, because they are often good sources of short feature articles and biographies.
5. Browse the daily paper *USA Today* and magazines such as *Discovery*, *Newsweek*, *Scientific American*, and *Consumer Reports*, because these publications often have articles with interesting graphics and charts. In addition to serving as reading material, such pieces can serve as good models for nonfiction writing by students.

6. Get familiar with edited collections of essays, poetry, and short stories. Our favorites include the *Chicken Soup for the Soul* series and annual series such as *The Best American Short Stories* and *Best American Essays*.

7. Consult lists of books for young adults that have received honors, such as the Coretta Scott King Award (*www.ala.org/srrt/csking/index.html*), the Pura Belpre Award (*www.ala.org/alsc/belpre.html*), or Notable Books for a Global Society (*www.csulb.edu/org/childrens-lit/index.html*). Except for the Young Adults' Choice Awards (*www.reading.org/choices/index.html*), most of these honors were given by adults, not by adolescent readers themselves, so choose with caution.

8. Read the student-authored book reviews and message board postings at *www.teenreads.com*, a website devoted to young people's reading. You may also want to read reviews of books for young people at *www.amazon.com* or *www.barnesandnoble.com*.

9. Make a habit of browsing websites such as *www.msnbc.com* and *www.cnn.com* for articles on breaking news. You may want to note the URL address and read the articles with your tutee online, where links to other articles will be available.

10. Search the websites of government agencies and organizations for primary sources such as letters, diaries, official documents, and maps (see Figure 6.3 for some sites that tutors often find useful).

The Census Bureau (*www.census.gov*)

This site is a terrific source for demographic data presented in documents such as maps, tables, and charts. It also includes lesson plans for teachers that could be adapted for tutoring.

Favorite Poem Project (*www.favoritepoem.org*)

The Web-based home for the project launched by former Poet Laureate Robert Pinsky, this site includes print texts and videotaped readings of individuals' favorite poems.

The Library of Congress (*www.loc.gov*)

Of particular interest is the section called "America's Library: Fun for Kids and Families." Other parts of the site offer access to digital collections of primary source documents from the United States and around the world.

National Aeronautics and Space Administration (*www.nasa.org*)

Be sure to visit NASA Kids, a section aimed at young people, which includes interviews, articles, and animated features on such topics as the space shuttle, weather, and meteors.

The Smithsonian (*www.smithsonian.org*)

In addition to links to 15 museums, the site includes online resources organized into three categories: art and design, history and culture, and science and technology.

FIGURE 6.3. Websites with short texts of interest to adolescents.

EVALUATING TEXTS FOR DIFFICULTY

Once you've identified your tutee's interests and located a range of reading material related to those interests, you still need to determine whether a particular text will be appropriate for use in a tutoring session. One of the best ways we know to do this is to read the text and make some notes about its features. We demonstrate that process here by analyzing Martin Luther King, Jr.'s, famous speech from 1963, "I Have a Dream." Just a bit more than 1,500 words, it qualifies as a short text, and it's very commonly read in American secondary schools. (You might choose to use it with your tutee, if she has expressed an interest in the civil rights movement or if that topic is being considered in her social studies class.) Although the text is available on a number of different websites, we recommend that you download it from the Martin Luther King Jr. Papers Project (*www.stanford.edu/group/king*), because this version is accurate and complete. You will probably want to print the text, so you can refer to it as you work your way through the rest of this chapter.

Readability

Before we turn to the specific features of this speech, however, we want to say a few words about readability formulas, because you may hear about them during your tutoring experience, especially if you're working in a school site. An estimate of how difficult a text is to read, *readability* is usually reported in terms of grade level (e.g., 7.3 means that the text should be appropriate for a typical reader in the third month of seventh grade). You've probably noticed figures like these on the back covers of books for children and young adults. Although there are different ways to calculate readability, the most common ones are based on the number of words per sentence and the number of syllables per word. Such a metric assumes that long sentences and words will be more difficult for readers to negotiate than shorter ones—an assumption that is often, though not universally, true.

If you use the computer program Microsoft Word (one that is readily available in many schools), you can obtain readability statistics for documents by using the following procedures: Type in the passage you want to evaluate, select Spelling and Grammar from the Tools menu, then click on the Options function of the Spelling and Grammar tool. Within the Options menu, check the box for Show Readability Statistics. After the document has been checked for grammar and spelling, a box will appear that summarizes these statistics and provides a grade level according to the Flesch–Kincaid formula. According to this formula, Martin Luther King, Jr.'s, "I Have a Dream" speech is written at the ninth-grade level.

A readability statistic can be very valuable to a tutor. For example, knowledge of it might prevent you from asking your seventh-grade tutee to read the text independently. You might think twice about using the text even with a ninth grader, if he struggles with reading. At the same time, you should use readability data cautiously, keeping in mind that such formulas don't take into consideration how much prior knowledge an individual reader brings to a text, nor whether the text is clearly written, coherently organized, or on an interesting topic (Allington,

2001). They also don't account for the support a tutor or teacher can provide readers during a lesson.

Student-Determined Levels of Difficulty

Another way to ascertain how difficult a particular text may be for a tutoring session is to talk to your student and see which reading materials she typically finds easy, just right, or challenging for her (Miller, 2002) and then to compare the text in question to those patterns and trends. Our own experience suggests that most middle school students would find Dr. King's speech to be "challenging," as would the majority of high school students likely to be designated for literacy tutoring. But because adolescents differ in their interests, background knowledge, and skill level, you will want to gather more specific data about perceived text difficulty from your particular student. In Chapter 4, we talked about asking your student to read a portion of the text aloud while you keep track of his errors. We recommended that you ask your student to deal independently with only those materials he could read at 95% accuracy or better. We suggested that texts for instruction—the ones you might use to demonstrate a new strategy—should be those the student can read with between 90 and 94% accuracy.

Another way to attend to text difficulty for your particular student is to pursue materials selection collaboratively. In our recommendations for your first tutoring session in Chapter 5, we suggested that you spend some time browsing books together in the school or public library. In addition to offering an unintimidating way of getting to know each other, such a session can help you identify some texts together that could be used in subsequent tutoring sessions. As you interact with your tutee in the library, pay close attention to what materials she selects and ask her to talk with you about how difficult she believes each text is likely to be for her. At this time, it may be useful to share some information about your own reading habits and preferences, to make it clear to your tutee that all readers, not just students, choose both easy and challenging material from time to time in addition to those "just right" texts that are most comfortable for them. Such disclosure may help your student feel more comfortable talking frankly about the texts with which she struggles as well as the texts she enjoys that might appear to be below grade level or "babyish." Conversations like these can establish baseline data about your tutee that you can use in your subsequent planning and materials selection. For this reason, we suggest that you keep notes about these conversations and add to these records as you spend more time with your tutee and gather additional data about her preferences, strengths, and needs.

Supports and Challenges

A third way to think about what kinds of difficulties a particular text may present to your tutee is to evaluate that text carefully in terms of its supports and challenges. A *support*, quite simply, is defined as any aspect or feature of a text that is likely to help the reader understand it. A *challenge* is just the opposite: any aspect or feature of a text that is likely to get in the way of the reader's comprehension. Typical supports might include the following:

- Definitions for difficult vocabulary that appear in parentheses after the word
- Pictures that illustrate key concepts clearly, often with captions
- Chapter and section headings that preview important ideas
- Short paragraphs with easily identified topic sentences
- Signals such as "The most important factor was" or "As a result of"

Typical challenges might include:

- Technical jargon that is not defined
- Complex diagrams with confusing labels or captions
- Long paragraphs with implicit topic sentences
- "Academic" language that is very different from the way students speak
- A lack of examples to support points that would be familiar to readers, given their experience with the topic

Keep in mind that this list only considers some of the supports and challenges a text *might* present. Knowledge of individual readers is necessary to determine whether a given aspect of the text will actually be a support or a challenge. Sometimes a feature may help one reader but hinder another. For example, a diagram with a color key in a science textbook might serve as a support to a visual learner, but it could be a challenge to a learner who relies more on verbal information. You'll need to know something about both the text and the reader to make the most informed evaluation. (This is where those early conversations in the library and your observational notes from your sessions can be very helpful.)

Generally speaking, students can read texts on their own that present more supports than challenges (these texts are likely to be the same ones your student identifies as "easy"). Texts that present roughly the same degree of challenge and support (those that are "just right") will serve you well as instructional material for tutor think-alouds, shared reading between the tutor and tutee, or other approaches that will allow you, the proficient reader, to model some aspect of the learning process for students. We don't recommend using many texts that present significantly more challenges than supports with the kinds of learners you'll be tutoring, because they are not likely to support fluent, expressive reading or the use of strategies. Remember, too, as you weigh supports against challenges that the equation isn't simply a numerical one (e.g., "I identified five supports and only three challenges, so this must be easy enough for my tutee to read on his own"). Instead, you'll need to think about how significant each of those supports and challenges is likely to be for your tutee. For example, a text may be too difficult for your tutee if it is littered with undefined, unfamiliar vocabulary, even if that's the only challenge you identify. The idea behind evaluating supports and challenges is to give you a framework for decision making (see Figure 6.4 for a summary), not a foolproof formula.

To help you think about these ideas more concretely, Figure 6.5 summarizes potential supports and challenges for King's "I Have a Dream" speech. Our two-column analysis suggests that King's speech is likely to be fairly difficult for the typical middle or even high school student. Although readers may have a little

Supports > Challenges

Student can read the text independently, or with limited tutor support.

Supports = Challenges

Tutor and student can read the text together, with the tutor modeling some aspect of reading process and the tutee taking on some responsibility for part of the text.

Supports < Challenges

Tutor should consider another text or, if the text is required reading, read it aloud to the tutee.

FIGURE 6.4. Decision-making framework for supports and challenges.

background knowledge about the civil rights movement, they will probably not be familiar with the details described in the speech. Because the text is an original, primary source (one composed by King himself) rather than a textbook description, readers will need to situate it in a context on their own, without much scene setting from the author. The vocabulary demands are also significant. We doubt that most adolescents, especially the kind in need of literacy tutoring, could read this text independently, unless they possessed a fair amount of prior knowledge from previous reading or instruction related to the civil rights movement. At the same time, the text is important enough to our history and includes enough supportive features that we would probably not reject it outright as a potential text for tutoring.

    We would be most likely to use this text as the basis for a tutor think-aloud. If you chose to use it with your student, you would then read it aloud, stopping peri-

Potential supports	Potential challenges
• On a topic about which most readers will most likely have some prior knowledge • Includes details of injustices done to African Americans at this time that should be of interest to adolescents • Uses short paragraphs in several sections • Repeats key phrases ("I have a dream that . . . ," "Let freedom ring"), making the text more predictable to reader • Includes an extended metaphor of the United States's "bad check" for African Americans that may make abstract concepts about justice and equity more accessible and familiar	• Requires reader to make some inferences where points aren't made explicitly (e.g., that Abraham Lincoln was the "great American" in the first paragraph) • Requires reader to have knowledge about the historical/political context in which the speech was made • Includes a good deal of unfamiliar vocabulary (e.g., *decree, manacles, defaulted, hallowed,* etc.). • Includes an extended metaphor (e.g., the United States's "bad check" for African Americans) that may not work for readers who know little about how checks and promissory notes work

FIGURE 6.5. An analysis of supports and challenges for King's "I Have a Dream" speech.

odically to share aspects of your thinking process with your tutee. More specifically, you could show him how to connect to relevant background knowledge or how to deal with unfamiliar words as you encounter them in context. It might be useful to read some or all of a picture-book biography of King beforehand, to ensure that your student has some basic information about him and his times. When you come to the parts of the text that follow a predictable pattern, you could invite your student to read along with you, either chorally (i.e., at the same time you read) or alternating sections with you. Each of these approaches would build on one or more of the supports we've identified in the text; each would make the challenges less of a hindrance to understanding the speech. This, from our perspective, is the goal of evaluating supports and challenges in text: determining whether the text is appropriate for your tutee or not, and if it is appropriate, deciding how to approach it together.

CONNECTING TO REQUIRED CURRICULA

Occasionally, you may be asked by your tutee or a teacher to work through an assigned reading, such as a chapter in the biology textbook. Tutoring centered on such a text can help adolescents learn to be more strategic readers as well as aid them in learning new content—topics we address in more depth in the next chapter. It's important to note, however, that there are other ways to connect to required curricula that don't require you and your tutee to relinquish all of your power to select texts. As we mentioned in Chapter 3, try to guard against turning your literacy-focused tutoring sessions into homework help.

One way to avoid this trap is to select texts with your tutee that supplement the curriculum but have not been assigned by his teacher. Adolescents often struggle with assigned reading because they lack necessary background knowledge about the topic. Tutoring sessions can help build this knowledge in a supportive environment. Students who have encountered key concepts and vocabulary in "reader-friendly" texts during tutoring will be better equipped to deal with them later in more challenging assignments in class. For example, reading excerpts from a nonfiction book for young people such as *Mistakes That Worked* (Jones, 1991) may pique your tutee's interest and develop his knowledge base for a science unit on inventions and inventors. The experience he gains with this related text during tutoring may help him to make predictions—an important active reading strategy—as he reads the required text, and it will most likely build his confidence, too.

Similarly, you may choose to read additional texts on a topic already covered in class, as a way to reinforce that knowledge and develop strategies with familiar content. Eileen Kenny, a preservice social studies teacher, used this approach while serving as a literacy tutor to an eighth grader named Justin. After Justin's class read a *Scholastic Scope* article on the treatment of women in Third World countries, Eileen selected an article on Afghan women from a current issue of *Newsweek*. According to Eileen, she decided to use the second piece "because Justin said he liked learning about other cultures and it was similar to what he read in class." By selecting a text that connected Justin's interests and his class curriculum, Eileen provided him with the opportunity to be more successful as a reader as well as to make text-to-text comparisons—another important strategy that proficient readers use.

CONCLUDING THOUGHTS

Text selection and evaluation can be tricky. Even experienced teachers make mistakes, on occasion, asking students to negotiate material that is too difficult or that fails to engage them. Expect that you won't be perfect at this task from the start, and give yourself some license to experiment while gathering data from ongoing conversations with your tutee. As you get to know your student better, we predict it will become easier for you to make text selections. Many tutors find that locating the perfect text for a session—one that connects to a passion the learner has and matches her skill level—is one of the most satisfying aspects of their work.

CHAPTER 7

Tutoring Sessions on Comprehension

Julie Schopp could tell that her tutee understood the gist of what she was reading as they shared a novel together. Yet it seemed that the details of the book escaped her. Reading, for this young woman, seemed to mean sounding out words and figuring out what they meant in only a very general way. Julie decided to complete a series of lessons to help her student do a better job of visualizing the text's vivid descriptions as a way to begin to foster her comprehension. Such visualization helps us to read between the lines of a text, that is, to draw inferences about what is not written. Julie noted the following about her work with her student:

> "Our session on October 17th dealt with visualization from the book *The Witch of Blackbird Pond*. The passage I chose dealt with Kit bringing gifts to her cousins from Barbados. Elizabeth George Speare vividly described the gorgeous dresses and embroidered gloves that Kit presented. I asked Ashley to close her eyes and just picture what I was reading in her head. In one excerpt I read out loud, Kit was described as giving a 'peacock blue petticoat' to Mercy. At the end of the passage, I asked Ashley to look around and show me a color she saw in her head that resembled the peacock blue. Since we were in the library, there were many posters and books full of different shades of colors."

The preceding example demonstrates an important concept in teaching reading comprehension: guided practice, a middle step on the way to gradual release of responsibility (Pearson & Gallagher, 1983). As we described in Chapter 2, gradual release begins when a teacher models an important aspect of reading so that a learner can see how the strategy works—in Julie's case, visualization. The teacher then invites the learner to try it for herself, with help and support, as Julie did with her tutee. The demonstration is complete when a teacher and learner discuss varying applications of the strategy, and the learner actually tries it for herself when reading other texts, perhaps writing mental pictures on a Post-It note as she reads, so that her teacher can keep track of her thinking.

Comprehension is the point of reading, and, thus, the aspect of reading that is of most concern to adolescents who will soon graduate from high school. Amplifying ideas that were introduced in Chapter 2, this chapter contains important information about helping your adolescent tutee to develop comprehension strategies for reading a variety of texts. It also contains tutoring ideas to help students whose lack of skill with decoding or lack of fluency gets in the way of their ability to comprehend.

TEACHING TUTEES WHAT GOOD READERS KNOW ABOUT COMPREHENSION

Reading comprehension requires action on the part of readers, and, as you know from your own reading, we use a variety of strategies to construct meaning while reading. Much research suggests that effective teachers of comprehension are those who design lessons that explicitly teach various aspects of the reading comprehension process, with attention to gradual release of responsibility (described in more detail in Chapter 2).

The course of the gradual release process varies among learners. Most learners require a great deal of modeling and guided practice over time in order to learn a particular comprehension strategy. Most learners also require an additional round of modeling when they find themselves working in unfamiliar contexts, such as when they engage in the varied reading required across the curriculum. Some learners require more help with some strategies and contexts than others, though. Some will remember how to use some of the strategies you suggest but will need reminders or even mnemonic devices in order to move themselves toward greater independence. One-on-one (or two-on-one) tutoring provides an ideal context for noting such needs in learners and responding accordingly.

Be careful, however! One-on-one work also provides a context within which a learner can learn to depend too much on a tutor for reading comprehension. Tutors need to remind themselves and their learners of this pitfall, and they need to talk with students about reaching a time when they will actually use a reading strategy on their own and outside the tutoring sessions. Working with young adults makes this a bit easier than it is with younger learners. Talk with your tutee about what he needs to do to use a strategy without you, and ask him to repeat it to you and to describe applications. Talk, too, about how to cope with especially difficult texts. Sometimes even rehearsing steps, and getting your tutee to do the same, can be helpful for this purpose. To this end, you might ask your tutee questions such as the following:

What connections to your life can you make with this material?
How can you make pictures in your mind as you read?
What should we do when we're having trouble understanding a text?

- Make connections between what they're reading and their own lives, other texts, and the world around them.
- Ask themselves questions as they read.
- Visualize as they read and make inferences, or informed guesses, that go beyond the information stated explicitly in the text.
- Determine what information is most important in a text, given their purpose for reading.
- Monitor when their understanding breaks down and take steps to repair it.

FIGURE 7.1. What good readers do.

Figure 7.1 provides an overview of six comprehension strategies typically used by proficient readers: making connections, questioning, visualizing, making inferences, determining importance, and monitoring/repairing comprehension when it breaks down. Each of these strategies and the instructional approaches that promote them are described below.

Making Connections

As we read, we make connections between what we're reading and our own lives, other texts, and the world around us (Dole et al., 1991). For instance, if we read, say, a biology text on the differences between bacterial and viral infections, we might make connections to various illnesses we've had over time, ranging from bacterial illnesses such as strep throat to viral ones such as the common cold. We might also read a text that invites the comparison of ancient Greek democracy to the more familiar model of democracy in the United States. Reading a theorem in mathematics class might trigger a connection to a previously read theorem.

Think: What Do I Already Know about This Topic?

Readers often make such connections automatically, although some do not. In either case, it can be helpful to call this strategy to your tutee's attention as a means of increasing insights regarding a particular text. One very helpful tutoring strategy involves asking your learner to review the title, headings, and illustrations prior to the reading of a text. Then talk with your tutee about connections she might be able to make to previous experiences, texts read, or topics studied. Ask her to make predictions and then read together to refine the predictions by section. Help her to strive for connections that make sense and that are refined continually to facilitate comprehension of the particular text in question. Such activation of prior knowledge can be really helpful to reading comprehension (McKeown, Beck, & Sinatra, 1992).

This Reminds Me of . . .

Ellen Keene and Susan Zimmermann (1997) reported a way to promote the identification of such connections that many, many teachers we know have found helpful. Grab some Post-It notes and explain to your tutee that good readers make three types of connections in order to make sense of a text: *text-to-text* (connections among ideas contained in texts they have read); *text-to-self* (connections to things they have been thinking about); and *text-to-world* connections. Then read a paragraph aloud and note a connection that you make as you finish your reading, beginning with language such as, "This reminds me of . . ." and finishing the sentence with an example of how you make text-to-text, text-to-self, or text-to-world connections. As you do this, write *TT*, *TS*, or *TW* on a Post-It and paste your note into the text. Hand a blank Post-It to your learner, and ask him what connection he can make, helping him to make a similar notation. Repeat the process over time, in different kinds of fiction and nonfiction texts.

Some adolescents have difficulty making connections because they think they know little about the subject they are reading, and sometimes this concern is true. But at other times, brief conversations reveal connections the reader did not originally see (e.g., he might say, "I don't know anything about DNA, but I know about the traits I inherited from my father"). Tutoring provides a great context for such conversation.

Kathy once watched two high school students struggle with understanding a brief assignment in their global history book as they worked with a tutor. The passages described feudalism. The tutor literally translated the reading, drawing a diagram of a manor, showing locations of the lord's house, knights' quarters, serfs' huts, shops, and farmland. Only when the tutor answered the query "What's a serf?" with the reply "Like a slave of the manor" did the two youths' eyes show a glint of recognition, having made a connection. Their dialogue provided a context within which the tutor could help the students make connections.

Another thing this tutor could have done to help his tutees build additional background knowledge was to use simpler text sources about feudalism. For instance, a trip to the library could have provided access to other books that described feudal times with colorful illustrations. Such texts as Jane Bingham's *Usborne World History: Medieval Times* can be useful in helping readers build background knowledge about medieval times.

A virtual trip to the World Wide Web could also locate more easily read explanations on many topics. A website such as the Manchester Medieval Portal (*www.medievalsources.co.uk*) could provide helpful additional information on feudalism. Searching for information with your tutee would be ideal, because you can demonstrate searching strategies for her. During your sessions you can talk about how you located your supplemental Web-based texts for tutoring, even if you and your tutee are not at an Internet-connected place and cannot search for additional information together.

Questioning

We ask ourselves questions as we read (Singer & Donlan, 1989). We are aware of some of these questions, especially those we ask to resolve problems raised by reading. We are unaware of others. For instance, consider those almost-unconscious questions that propel us through a good book or interesting newspaper article, such as "What made the author mention that location twice? It must be important," or "I wonder who the reporter's unnamed source was for that information." Indeed, as Harvey and Goudvis (2000) suggest, "A reader with no questions might as well abandon the [text]" (p. 82).

We might ask ourselves questions about how one section of a text connects to something else we know (e.g., "How does this discussion of mitosis and meiosis connect to what I already know about reproduction?"). We might also ask questions about something going on in a story (e.g., "Why is this character being so mean to her sister?"). We might ask questions about something we don't understand, prompting us to reread earlier sections of a text (e.g., "What is a sedimentary rock?") or propelling us ahead (e.g., "What *is* going to happen next?"). When we don't have questions—say, because a teacher assigned the reading—good readers work with the text to figure out what they can, and are supposed to, get from it, given the teacher's assignment. Tutors should model their own questioning while reading, including what to do when reading texts one might not choose on one's own. Figure 7.2 includes a tutor's think-aloud demonstrating this self-questioning process with Steve Jenkins's (2002) *Life on Earth*, a nonfiction text about evolution—a topic that is often difficult for young people to understand from a textbook depiction.

In *Strategies That Work: Teaching Comprehension to Enhance Understanding*, Stephanie Harvey and Anne Goudvis (2000) explain that they like to teach learners to develop "thick" and "thin" questions as they read. Thick questions are global questions that address universal concepts (e.g., I wonder . . . , Why . . . ?, How come . . . ?) or large content areas (e.g., What is weathering?). They note that the answers to these questions often "are long and involved, and require further discussion and research" (p. 90). On the other hand, thin questions address simple confusions, vocabulary, or specific content and can be answered with simple answers, definitions, or yes/no responses.

Harvey and Goudvis describe a teacher who asks students to use different-sized Post-It notes for thick and thin questions, with larger ones reserved for thick questions. This teacher has students read a section of text, write a question on the front of the Post-It, and then note the answer on the back. The different-sized notes can help a learner to see the kinds of questions he has, overall, about a passage, perhaps letting him know if a trip to the library for further background reading is in order when a lot of larger notes protrude from a text after completing an assignment. Kathy has even observed teachers organize riveting whole-class discussions around questions students generated while reading. The teacher mediated the discussion as students put their notes on a white board, referring to them as they helped each other answer some questions and look for answers to others.

Taffy Raphael (1984) also described a categorical scheme for question-and-answer relationships that might be helpful for your tutee to use as she tries to find answers to her questions. Raphael described "right there questions" as those that can be answered by pointing to information directly stated in the text. "Think and search questions" are those that can be answered by reading between the lines—drawing inferences from what is said in a text about something that is not stated directly. "On your own questions" refer to the text but also require that learners consider their opinions about a topic related to the text. Of course, readers may construct any kind of questions in order to fulfill their purposes for reading. Raphael's categories can provide a helpful framework for a tutor and tutee to use in generating questions or considering questions that teachers might ask later.

Kim's general biology class has begun to study the topic of evolution, and Kim's teacher reported to her tutor, Julia, that Kim's quiz scores suggest that she is struggling with the textbook chapter. Julia decides to develop a tutoring lesson around an easier text on this topic that will provide Kim with background information she can use in class, as well as develop the valuable comprehension strategy of questioning. After perusing some resources on the subject, she selects Steve Jenkins's *Life on Earth* (2002), a scientifically accurate non-fiction picture book with vivid, accessible language and striking illustrations. After she shows the book to Kim, Julia explains that the focus of their lesson will be on questioning, a strategy readers use to help them stay actively engaged in the text. She tells Kim that she will think aloud to show her what kinds of questions she is generating as she makes her way through a few pages.

JULIA: Kim, I'm going to read a little bit of the book and then stop to tell you what questions I have in my head. I'll look up at you when I'm thinking aloud, so it will be easier for you to tell what I'm reading and what I'm thinking. [Julia begins to read.] *In 1831 a ship named the Beagle left England to sail around the world on a scientific expedition. The scientist and naturalist Charles Darwin was aboard.* Who financed the expedition? You hear all the time about who financed explorations of the New World—for example, Queen Isabella of Spain and Columbus—but I don't think I know who would be financing a scientific expedition at this time. *Over the next five years, he observed and collected plants and animals from many parts of the world.* I didn't realize his expedition had taken so long. I wonder where they spent most of their time. *After he returned to England, he spent years studying what he had collected and thinking about the things he had seen. Finally, combining his own ideas with those of earlier scientists, he was able to develop the theory of evolution.* Who were those other scientists? I wonder if it says in the biology textbook.

OK, that's the first paragraph of this section. I think I'll keep going and question my way through another paragraph, then we can stop and talk about what we've read and what you've noticed about my questions. *On his voyage, Darwin visited the Galapagos, an isolated group of islands in the Pacific Ocean.* I wonder if the isolation was what made their specimens so useful. *There, among other unique forms of life, he found an unusual group of finches.* What is a finch, anyway? I think there might be some in central New York, but I'm not sure. I don't think they're very big birds, if they're the ones I'm thinking about. *These birds gave Darwin important clues about the way evolution works. He believed that all of the finches were the descendants of the same two birds, but he noticed that on each island the birds' beaks were shaped differently.* How did he know they were descendants of the same two birds? What made him think that? *The finches on each island ate different kinds of food, and Darwin believed that small changes in the birds over many generations had resulted in fourteen different species, each with a beak adapted to a particular diet.* It's kind of interesting to me that according to this book, Darwin's ideas about finches were the ones that really helped him put this theory together. A lot of times people associate Darwin with his ideas about humans descending from monkeys and apes. I wonder why this story about the finches is overlooked and the monkey one so much more emphasized.

Let's stop here and talk for a little. What did you notice about my questions, Kim? Why do you think those questions might be helpful to me as a reader?

FIGURE 7.2. A tutor's think-aloud on questioning the text. Quoted material in italic is from Jenkins (2002, pp. 20–21).

Visualizing and Inferring

Visualization helps reading comprehension (Gambrell & Jawitz, 1999). Even so, Kathy has come across a number of young readers who do not realize that good readers make pictures in their heads as they read, and then draw inferences about what is going on based on these pictures. Instead, these readers describe a reading process that consists mostly of pronouncing words. But as Julie Schopp showed us at the beginning of this chapter, good readers visualize and then make inferences, or informed guesses, that go beyond information stated explicitly in the text (Dole et al., 1991). They might visualize pictures that go along with a story, as Julie helped her tutee to do at this chapter's opening, and draw inferences about, in this case, what kind of setting was connoted by the wearing of a peacock-blue dress.

A tutor can help a tutee visualize and draw inferences in other ways. For example, you might ask your learner to look at a cover illustration to predict the content of a nonfiction text related to a social studies topic currently being studied, then to read and draw an inference about whether the prediction was, indeed, close to what was contained in the text. You might also ask your learner to draw pictures of what she reads or to create an illustration of something you read to her. Be careful here, though: some readers who struggle have figured out how to avoid reading by procrastinating on what should be quick sketches!

In *I Read It But I Don't Get It: Comprehension Strategies for Adolescent Readers*, Cris Tovani (2000) suggests helping readers to find those five or six words in a passage that really contribute to the imagery. They might be words that describe something, like the colors noted in Julie Schopp's journal entry at the beginning of the chapter. Important words might also be those that call to mind images in other texts, movies, or television shows. Looking for such words will focus your tutee's attention on the imagery of a particular text in important ways that she will be able to use later, when you are not present and she is having difficulty figuring out an author's intended imagery.

You can also help your tutee to learn to make inferences in some playful ways, perhaps by using short excerpts from feature films, which often require viewers to infer just as much as print texts do, or comic strips, which often depend on inference for their humor. Kathy Connors, an art education student, created a fun activity for her tutee that required him to predict and make inferences about the meaning of nonsense words embedded in passages about a meaningful context—a student's school life. According to Kathy's lesson plan, her rationale for the lesson was as follows:

> "When Jack was doing the quiz over the origami book last week, I realized that he can take notes right from the text, but he could not necessarily infer answers he hadn't written down. The two answers he got wrong could have been inferred based on the reading. I thought I would try an exercise dealing with this topic. Hopefully, this will give him more experience making predictions and using information in a text to make educated guesses."

The worksheet Kathy created to guide her tutee's predictions and inferences appears in Figure 7.3. Note, as you read it, how Kathy's third example was more difficult than her first two, requiring her tutee to manage more unknown words after he had a chance to become familiar with the demands of the task.

You should help your learner to practice visualizing and inferring with both fiction and nonfiction texts. Include attention to textbooks—especially if you are working with a high school student; such texts are notoriously devoid of well-explained visual images and deserve extra attention in this area. Keeping in mind the principle of gradual release, you should explain that making mental pictures helps us determine what may not be directly stated in a text, making it clear that many authors would rather show than tell about settings and what they looked like. Model the strategy often, and invite your learner to join in with your brainstorming.

Determining Importance

Some adolescents are used to getting by with only a general sense of the meaning carried in a text selection. These youths depend on classroom discussion to explain details needed for tests. Teachers exacerbate this practice when they don't refer to the text, fail to depend on it as an information source, or use a text that is especially difficult or poorly written. One of Kathy's high school tutees had a teacher who told her that he hated the new textbook and based most of his lecture on the old one—even as he asked students to read a chapter in the new text for homework.

Good readers determine what information is most important in a text, given their purpose for reading (Winograd, 1984). Indeed, we determine importance in relation to our purposes and understandings, even when a teacher isn't asking us to do so. Most adolescent learners are able to note a key topic or idea from a text that you have read to them or that they have read for themselves. However, many youths need practice providing sufficient detail for learning tasks designated by a teacher or for the reading purposes they have set for themselves. You will want to teach your tutee how to determine importance, given varying purposes as well as the varying ways we have of noting importance, whether it is by writing summaries, drawing diagrams, or identifying important vocabulary terms. Read a common section of text and then think aloud as you restate important ideas and their supporting details.

Harvey and Goudvis (2000) remind us that there are often several important ideas in a given text selection rather than one main idea. Older students may have heard teachers use instructions such as "find the gist," "identify the topic," "locate the thesis sentence," "determine the main theme," and "summarize the main point," and mistakenly inferred that each selection has only one main idea. They may wonder why they feel like they are guessing what is in the teacher's head when other students produce teacher-approved responses that are longer or shorter, or more or less complex, than what they, themselves, were thinking. You will want to help your learner sort out such statements and learn that the idea of "what's important" really depends on the person's purpose for reading as much as on the author's intent. Help your learner see that good readers develop a sense of what's important in a text.

Read these journal entries from students talking about their day at school. Try to infer what the imaginary words really mean by reading. List your predictions of the words' meanings in the boxes provided. Feel free to add or cross out predictions until you feel you have found the real word.

I lost my *rasod*! I brought it home last night to study. I think I brought it with me to school. Maybe I left it on the bus? I can use one from another class for the rest of the day, but I need my notes from last week's class. I will have to ask the bus driver on the way home to see if he found it. If not, I will have to copy my friend's into a new *rasod*. I am always losing my stuff!

Predictions:

I have *nitsud* practice after school today. We have a game later this week. My mom used to play *nitsud*, too, so she likes to come to my games. Our goalie is home sick today, I wonder what our coach will do without her? I left my cleats in my locker; I will have to go get them after class or I cannot go to practice. I received the MVP our last game because I scored the *nitsud* ball with my head! I love this game!

Predictions:

I slept in too late this morning because my *tumaz* broke. I was late for the *yuka*. When I finally got to school, I went to see my *goomap*, but no one was in the room. I wandered the hallway looking into different classrooms. I went to the main office to ask for help. I saw the *tumaz* and realized that we were still in first block. Where was my class? The principle said that my *goomap* was in the *frafnob* with the rest of my class. She asked why I was late, and I told her how I had to walk to school. I went down the hallway to the *frafnob* to look for my *goomap*. When I got there, the class was looking for books for a research project. The *goomap* came to me and asked me where I had been. I told her about my *tumaz*, the *yuka*, and how I had been looking for the class. She laughed and said, "I guess it's time for a new *tumaz*!"

Tumaz	Yuka

Goomap	Frafnob

FIGURE 7.3. One tutor's activity to promote prediction and inferring.

Summarizing

When we want to tell someone about something we have read, or we need to remember it later, we summarize it. That is, we tell someone the essence of the idea in question, without including a lot of additional detail. A summary is not the same as a retelling (retellings include far more information), and it is important to help learners to see the difference between the two. A summary of a narrative story usually includes a reference to setting, time, characters, problem, and solution. A summary of a piece of expository text also usually includes some reference to the high points, given the organization of text. That is, a text might be organized to reflect causes and effects, a certain chronology, or a comparison–contrast of two related concepts in support of a set of important ideas.

In fact, it is useful to ask your tutee to summarize after each section of text that you complete together; this is especially appropriate when reading textbooks and other nonfiction work. Vacca and Vacca (2002) suggest that effective summarizers learn to integrate key words and topic sentences as the basis for drafting a summary of a section of text. In a tutoring dyad, you can do this by first brainstorming a list of key ideas and refining the list to only the most important ideas. Then search for a topic sentence, one that represents all the key ideas of a passage. Finally, draft a summary of the desired length that combines these two sources of information. For some learners, it may be helpful to begin with summarizing nonprint sources, such as television shows or movies.

Consideration of Various Kinds of Texts

One tutor we know gathered a pile of picture books to work with a ninth grader who seemed to be struggling with determining importance. He began by using *The Bracelet* (Uchida, 1993), *Thank You, Mr. Falker* (Polacco, 1998), and *Rose Blanche* (Innocenti, 1991)—all compelling stories. He and his tutee read these aloud together, each reading a page in turn; as picture books, they were finished quickly. After each, they talked together about which ideas were most important to the stories overall. For the first text, *The Bracelet*, they determined that the important idea was that Japanese Americans were unfairly interred during World War II. For *Thank You, Mr. Falker*, they realized that the text was about how even a reader who feels very unaccomplished can learn to read with the help of a caring and diligent teacher. Finally, they agreed that *Rose Blanche* was about how racism determined some children's fate in chilling ways.

They then worked with such equally compelling nonfiction picture books as *The Faithful Elephants* (Tsuchiya, 1988), *The Unbreakable Code* (Hunter, 1996), and *The Story of Ruby Bridges* (Coles, 1995), discussing the importance of one section of the texts at a time. Finally, they moved along to textbooks, having the same sorts of discussions as they read sections of text together, then comparing their lists of important ideas to what was said in the introductions and summaries of the texts. As they worked, the dyad had many, albeit brief, discussions about the differences in background that they brought to their reading, and about how their statements of the main idea sometimes differed from one another in subtle ways that might both be correct statements of the main idea. They even looked at some sample reading comprehension tests, realizing together that when a question asks you to determine importance, you should do so and then look for some version of your response among the multiple choices—rather than stabbing at a guess from the choices.

Constructing Graphic Organizers

The National Reading Panel (2000) reported that graphic organizers enhance readers' attention to a text's meaning. These diagrammatic arrangements of key concepts show relationships among ideas. Such diagrams can help a reader sort out which ideas are important and which are less so (Hyerle, 1996; Moline, 1995). Readers may draw graphic organizers to show relations among key ideas while reading sections of text. Writers may use them to outline a writing plan. You can model the use of graphic organizers for your tutee by reading aloud a section of text and then talking through key ideas as you draw a diagram of these (Barry, 2002; Fisher, Frey, & Williams, 2002). Show your learner typical illustrations, including those that identify main idea and supporting details, time lines, graphs, cause–effect relationships, compare–contrast tables, and flow charts (see Figure 7.4 for examples of two different graphic organizers; others can be found in Chapters 8 and 9).

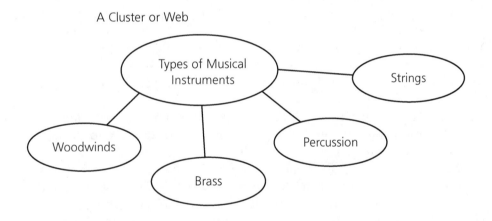

A Cluster or Web

A Semantic Feature Analysis

	Warm-blooded?	Vertebrate?	Breathes air?
Reptile	No	Yes	Yes
Amphibian	No	Yes	Yes (as adult)
Mammal	Yes	Yes	Yes
Fish	No	Yes	No

FIGURE 7.4. Sample graphic organizers.

Monitoring and Repairing Comprehension When It Breaks Down

Kathy was working with a young adult male a few years ago. She'd said, "So, when you're reading something you don't understand, you stop . . . and do what?" The young man looked at her incredulously and queried, "You're supposed to stop reading when you don't understand?" He had apparently struggled so much with reading prior to this exchange that he had come to think that it was appropriate to keep reading even when he did not understand. Many youths have come to believe that this is a personal weakness on their part, and that good readers always understand what they read.

Actually, nothing could be further from the truth! Good readers *don't* always understand what they read, but they do know what strategies to use when their understanding breaks down, and they do know how to take steps to repair it (Pearson & Fielding, 1994). Be sure that your tutee understands that good readers monitor their reading to ensure comprehension. Model by thinking aloud so that he knows what to do if he does not comprehend as well as he would like. Adolescents need to learn to ask themselves: "Did what I read just made sense to me?" They can attempt to summarize, and if they cannot do so because they do not understand what they have just read, they may do several things.

Show your tutee how good readers address their lack of understanding by rereading and by more consciously employing the comprehension strategies delineated earlier in this chapter. A characteristic of good readers is that they are confident they can solve the problem posed by their lack of comprehension of a particular text. Their response is to figure out the best way to deal with whatever problem arises. Students need to learn to take on the same problem-solving habits of mind when reading.

Depending on the circumstance, some readers may, indeed, decide to stop reading. From this point several different actions, known as fix-up strategies, may be taken. A reader who is not understanding as well as she would like may decide to reread the material and focus on making connections, asking questions, visualizing, or determining importance. Another reader might decide to pull out the difficult vocabulary words and work at figuring out their meaning, perhaps even drawing a graphic organizer to show relationships among apparent key ideas. Particular difficulty with text density—when words and sentences seem too long and jargon-filled to make sense—might cause some readers to leave a text and go to the Internet or other reference source and do some background reading. Still other readers might decide to plow ahead, actively asking questions and summarizing key ideas as they proceed, then rereading to gain a sense of what was meant by the problematic earlier passage.

THE IMPORTANCE OF MODELING STRATEGY INTEGRATION

Thus, after working with your tutee on the individual strategies discussed in earlier parts of this chapter, you will also want to work on helping her to consider the purposes of particular reading tasks in order to select from among a repertoire of strategies for completing such tasks. At this stage of independence, it can be helpful to list strategies and discuss how to make such choices, based on your own skills at purpose setting and strategic reading (e.g., "When I have to read things like this, I . . ."). It can be helpful to construct memory aids such as acronyms (e.g., QICMI for *q*uestion, *i*mage, *c*onnect, *m*onitor, *i*mportance) or sentences whose first initials give clues to strategies as memory aids. These can be noted for reference on an index card your tutee can use as a bookmark. One tutor addressed this important instructional need by revisiting strategies used to solve all the problems posed by reading. She modeled fix-up strategies for her learner and then repeatedly talked with her tutee about them. Another tutor, Trina Nocerino, reported:

> "My content—three fix-up strategies—was infused with casual dialogue and meaningful questions. I always tied our discussion back to the strategy, 'What did we just do? What information did we use to understand the reading?' "

Developed by Palinscar and Brown (1984), reciprocal teaching provides an excellent model of integrated use of reading comprehension strategies taught through gradual release of responsibility (see Figure 7.5 for an overview of the steps). The four reading comprehension strategies that are part of reciprocal teaching include predicting, generating questions, clarifying, and summarizing— all strategies reminiscent of those presented earlier in this chapter. Model each strategy in isolation initially, thinking aloud so your tutor can see how each works. Then invite your tutee to take turns with you, assuming your "teacherly" role in thinking through a particular strategy application aloud. Once each strategy has been modeled in turn, read aloud a passage, modeling integration of all the strategies. Again, invite your tutee to take turns with you, as you think aloud for each other, discussing questions and making predictions, clarifications, and summaries.

After you have thoroughly demonstrated each of the steps of this process, you should invite your student to alternate using them with you. Explain that these strategies are among the most common used by proficient readers. If you have two tutees, you could have each student alternate with each other as well as you.

- *Predict* from the title, subheading, or previous content you've read what you believe the next part of the text will be about.
- *Ask questions* that you have about the text as you read or that someone might ask you (e.g., a teacher on a quiz, a friend interested in the topic) after you finish.
- As you encounter words or parts of the texts that are confusing, stop and try to *clarify* them by talking about them.
- At the end of the section or text, *summarize* the most important ideas from your perspective.

FIGURE 7.5. Steps of reciprocal teaching. From *Tools for Teaching Content Literacy* by Janet Allen, copyright © 2004, with permission of Stenhouse Publishers.

CONCLUDING THOUGHTS

This chapter included information meant to support you as you help your adolescent tutee develop reading comprehension strategies. Here we revisit the idea that you will need to model the strategies good readers use to construct meaning using gradual release of responsibility. A variety of ways for you to explain and practice the details involved in such strategies is provided.

We also suggest that you focus your tutoring sessions on teaching your tutee to apply strategies during silent reading, because this is what we are required to do increasingly as we reach adulthood. We have suggested throughout this and other chapters that you and your tutee may want to use trade books, textbooks, or Internet sources for your reading materials. You may also want to use reading that is assigned for homework if it is available to you, and if you can be sure to have access to needed texts. Because you should try to keep yourself focused on a few strategies, over time, as you plot your course with your learner, you will want to use this assigned reading to serve your ongoing goals and objectives rather than to merely help the student can complete his homework.

CHAPTER 8

Tutoring Sessions on Writing

Recently, Kelly and a colleague conducted a study of adolescents' use of technology in their reading and writing (Chandler-Olcott & Mahar, 2003). Rhiannon, one of the girls who participated in the project, shared with Kelly how important writing was to her daily life: in addition to developing her own Web pages, she sent e-mail messages to friends and composed "fanfictions" (i.e., original stories using characters and settings from popular media texts). She was convinced, however, that her English teacher didn't like the writing she did in school, because she put "bad comments on my papers." Although Rhiannon felt that her teacher's perceptions were due to her limited viewpoint ("She only sees the essay part of my writing, which doesn't help"), she chose not to share her fanfictions in class, because she believed her teacher would neither understand nor appreciate them.

Rhiannon's example suggests some principles for you to consider when working with your tutee on his writing. First, identify his strengths as a writer and be sure that he is aware of them, too. Rhiannon resisted her teacher's feedback because she believed—correctly or not—that her teacher focused on the deficiencies of her work, not its successes. As you tutor, do remember that people often feel exposed and vulnerable when sharing their writing; it's not an easy thing to do. Pointing out your tutee's strengths as a writer first, before you begin to deal with his needs, will help to put him at ease (a social benefit), and it may also help him cognitively, making him aware of the positive aspects of his writing so that he can keep doing them.

Second, take Lucy Calkins's (1986) advice to "Teach the writer, not the writing." As a tutor, you may be tempted to "fix" a piece of writing by pointing out all the things that are wrong with it. Perhaps you have received papers from your own teachers that were littered with the kind of "bad comments" in the margins that Rhiannon reports. Although it is important to provide honest response to students (we're not suggesting that you tell them their pieces are flawless when they're not), little research evidence exists to support the practice of marking each and every error a student makes (Weaver, 1996). Instead, writers tend to make the most progress when their teachers zero in on one or two areas for improvement in a piece, providing face-to-face instruction that can be generalized to other writing situations. The ultimate goal of tutoring is to help your student learn to use various strategies independently, not to help him create one or two "perfect" pieces.

Third, and finally, be aware that your tutee may have experience and interests as a writer that do not necessarily align with the opportunities he is given to write in school. Although Rhiannon did appear to struggle with formal academic writing, she, like many other teenagers, used literacy competently in various other contexts (Schultz, 2002). Unfortunately, her personal writing offered few opportunities for feedback and response from others, making it difficult for her to improve. Although your tutoring will probably be centered on helping your tutee acquire greater skill with the genres that dominate in schools and workplaces, opening up some space in your sessions for him to share and work on writing *he* values can help you assess his strengths, create a bond of trust between you, and foster strategies that he may be able to use in a number of writing situations in and out of school.

FROM THE WRITING PROCESS TO WRITING PROCESSES

If you spent even a little time in elementary classrooms during the 1980s or 1990s, chances are good that you saw a poster hanging on a wall that looked something like Figure 8.1. Classroom charts like these were inspired by studies showing that proficient writers use a series of reasonably predictable components when they compose (Graves, 1983; Murray, 1985). This research had a significant impact on daily practice for K–12th-grade students. Instead of simply assigning topics and grading the essays that resulted, as had been common in the past, teachers began to teach the writing process deliberately, providing short demonstrations on each component and conferring with students over their working drafts.

For the most part, these changes were positive. They increased the volume of writing students did, and they focused attention on aspects of composing that had rarely been formally taught to young learners. In some classrooms, however, the research on components of the writing process was translated into a numbered list of "steps" that students were encouraged—sometimes even required—to follow,

Step 1: Plan/brainstorm.

Step 2: Draft.

Step 3: Revise.

Step 4: Edit.

Step 5: Publish.

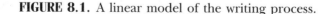

FIGURE 8.1. A linear model of the writing process.

without deviation. We have both heard stories from students in supposedly process-oriented classrooms who drafted an outline after the essay was completed as evidence of their "planning," or who created an artificially messy copy with cross-outs and corrections in order to receive full credit for editing an assignment. Far from promoting the development of the writing process as it occurs for real writers, these teachers' insistence that students follow each step just created new kinds of disconnected products.

The most current professional literature on writing instruction advocates teaching students how to orchestrate these various components but emphasizes the recursive, flexible nature of composing (Fletcher & Portalupi, 1998; Fountas & Pinnell, 2001). Teachers show their students multiple ways to approach, say, revision, so that individuals can choose what works for them. In fact, it's probably best to talk to students about writing process*es*, rather than The Writing Process, because the former emphasizes that writers approach tasks differently depending on their purposes and audiences. If you think about the nature of your own composing efforts, you'll probably realize that writers sometimes skip components (people don't usually edit grocery lists for spelling) or return to one component again and again (e.g., we often find when writing professional articles that we revise some sections many times before even beginning to draft others).

We encourage you to talk with your tutee about the processes he uses while writing. What does he know about the various components, and with which ones does he feel most comfortable? Does he know how to adjust his approach when encountering different writing tasks? What kinds of writing instruction has he received, and what did that instruction encourage him to value? You'll want to think about the same questions in regard to your own writing, because sharing your own processes honestly can be very useful to your student.

CONNECTING READING AND WRITING

Literacy researchers have long known that those processes traditionally known as the language arts—reading, writing, listening, and speaking—are interrelated (Gavelek et al., 2000). Content literacy researchers Vacca and Vacca (2002) make this case eloquently for reading and writing: "When reading and writing are taught in tandem, the union influences content learning in ways not possible when students read without writing or write without reading. When teachers invite a class to write before or after reading, they help students use writing to think about what they will read and to explore and think more deeply about the ideas they have read" (p. 246).

When Hana Zima, one of Kelly's students, tutored Michael, a struggling reader in seventh grade, one of her main goals was that he use writing to consider information in reading from a new angle. In one lesson, she used a nonfiction text about the history of football to tap into Michael's interest in sports. To help him contemplate what he had read, as well as to assess his understanding, she asked him to write informally about the first Super Bowl from whatever participant's perspective (coach, referee, player, fan) he chose. She also asked him to illustrate his brief composition—a choice that allowed Michael, a more confident artist than writer, to use one of his strengths.

One of Hana's classmates, Julie Schopp, used another instructional approach to connect reading and writing. The two sixth graders she tutored, Ashley and Alicia, had read the novel *Hello, My Name Is Scrambled Eggs* (Gilson, 1992) in their English language arts class. During a tutoring session, Julie asked them to construct a biopoem on one of the characters using the following structure from Gere (1985):

Line   1: First name
Line   2: Four traits that describe character
Line   3: Relative of ____
Line   4: Lover of ____
Line   5: Who feels ____ (three items)
Line   6: Who needs ____ (three items)
Line   7: Who fears ____ (three items)
Line   8: Who gives ____ (three items)
Line   9: Who would like to see ____ (three items)
Line 10: Resident of ____
Line 11: Last name

The biopoem was effective with Julie's students for several reasons. It allowed the girls some choice about which character to focus on—an approach that is generally more motivating than having the entire assignment specified. It served as a summarization tool, helping the girls to cement and reflect on their knowledge from the novel. It also allowed them to share that knowledge in a larger social context, as they read their completed poems aloud to the rest of their class when they returned from tutoring.

In addition to Hana's and Julie's approaches, you might consider the following possibilities for connecting reading and writing:

- Show your tutee how to make a three-column K-W-L chart (Ogle, 1986), two columns of which are completed before reading (what he *k*nows about the topic before reading and what he *w*ants to know), and one of which is completed after the selection has been completed (what he *l*earned). See Figure 8.2 for an example of one learner's K-W-L chart before and after reading a nonfiction selection on zoos.
- Invite your tutee to keep a reader response log for the texts you read together. You might prompt him to write a paragraph or two about his favorite part, to make connections to his own life, or to log questions that arise while reading.
- Write a review of a book together and post it to an online space such as *www.teenreads.com* or *www.amazon.com*.
- Read a text or a set of texts together, paying close attention to the author's style or organizational structure. Then help your tutee to use that model in his own writing.

What I **K**now	What I **W**ant to Know	What I **L**earned
• Some endangered species of animals exist only in zoos • Some zoos, like the one in San Diego, have very successful captive breeding programs • Zoo habitats are becoming more "naturalistic" in their design • Some animal-rights groups oppose zoos as inhumane	• How do zoos keep animals from cold climates (e.g., polar bears from the Arctic) in hot areas like the desert? • How do zoos get their animals in the first place? • How do zoos keep animals from getting bored?	• Animals on the verge of extinction are managed with their own SSPs (Species Survival Plans) • Successful captive breeding programs send babies and "extra" animals to other zoos that need them for their SSPs • Zoos develop enrichment programs, often with hidden food or toys, to keep animals from getting bored; some zoos label these attempts on their exhibits to educate the public about animal behavior

FIGURE 8.2. A K-W-L chart completed before and after reading a nonfiction selection on zoos.

SUGGESTIONS FOR STRATEGY-FOCUSED LESSONS

If you look at any of the popular resources for teachers of writing—for example, Ralph Fletcher and JoAnn Portalupi's *Craft Lessons* (1998)—you'll see lessons on how to write a catchy title, fashion a powerful opening paragraph, and capture a character with gesture. Lessons like these are interesting and useful to young writers, particularly when they take place in classrooms whose daily practices promote writing development. As a tutor, however, you will probably make the most impact on your student if you focus your efforts in the three "bread-and-butter" areas with which adolescent writers often struggle: planning and organization, development of details, and mastering the surface features or conventions of standard written English. This section provides concrete ideas for lessons in each of these areas.

Strategies for Planning and Organization

Many struggling adolescent writers have trouble organizing their thoughts for a composition. It's not that they don't have anything to say—sometimes, quite the opposite—but they often don't know how to get started or how to link their ideas in a logical progression. Tutoring can give them useful strategies in this area that they can then use for a variety of writing tasks.

The best writing assistance you provide for your tutee may not involve writing a single word. James Britton, a well-respected literacy researcher from Great Britain, coined the saying talk is "the sea upon which all else floats" (as cited in Vacca & Vacca, 2002, p. 214), to speak to writers' need to talk to others about their ideas, often long before they put pen to paper. Talking with an interested adult about their writing during tutoring can help adolescents (1) realize that what they're thinking is worth writing about, (2) decide on a topic, (3) settle on how to begin a piece, (4) determine an appropriate tone for the audience, (5) articulate their main idea or argument, and (6) plan how long the piece may need to be. Do not underestimate how valuable it can be to confer informally with your tutee, asking him to talk about his understandings of an assignment and helping him to develop a game plan for approaching that task.

More specifically, you may want to try one or more of the following approaches meant to help students plan and organize their thinking for writing:

- Introduce your tutee to the concept of "freewriting"—composing for 5–10 minutes without stopping or censoring one's ideas—on a topic as a way to "jump-start" her brain. Tell her that the two of you can organize the thoughts she generates from this process after she finishes writing; encourage her to ignore mistakes, repetitions, and false starts while trying to get as much on paper as possible.

- Show your tutee how to make a cluster or web of related ideas before writing (see Figure 8.3 for a sample cluster of reasons, drawing on a reading by Donald [1996], about why the North won the American Civil War). If your student is not familiar with this tool, we suggest modeling how to construct one yourself, followed by a demonstration of how to use the web to guide a first draft. Then, using the gradual release of responsibility model outlined in Chapter 2, you can construct another planning web together before your tutee has the opportunity to make one independently.

- Teach your student some note-taking strategies to keep track of ideas in her reading that she may want to use in a piece of writing. Many adolescents find a double-entry journal to be a useful tool for organizing their thinking. On the left side of the page, students record a direct quotation from the text that strikes them as important; on the right side of the page, they record notes about what that quotation means to them and why it is important. They can use these notes when they begin to draft an assignment that requires them to draw on examples from text.

- Develop a "skeleton" for the piece together, and then turn your student loose to complete it after some conversation with you. One tutor we know used this approach when working with a student who attended an alternative high school in Boston. He wanted to write a letter to his son, born a few months before the lesson, which would describe his hopes and dreams for the child. The tutor helped him to draft the greeting and the beginning sentence for each of the three paragraphs he wanted to write, then she left spaces between those sentences so that he could go back and develop those ideas on his own.

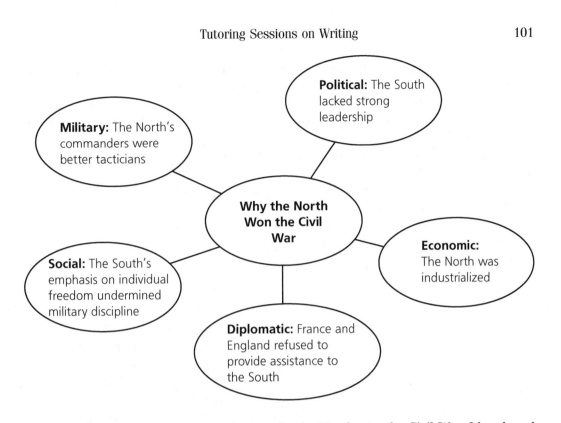

FIGURE 8.3. A sample cluster on reasons why the North won the Civil War. Ideas based on chapter titles in Donald (1996).

This last example leads us to a point we want to make about a teaching approach you may encounter if you are tutoring in a school site, particularly one where students have struggled with standardized tests. Called a "framed paragraph," this activity requires students to fill in blanks inserted into a number of sentences in a generic paragraph constructed by their teacher or a commercial publisher (e.g., "The most important event in my country's history was _____"). The idea is that students will internalize the key elements of a well-structured paragraph by inserting information from their individual inquiries into the spaces and copying over the entire paragraph. We tend to be skeptical about the effectiveness of this technique, even when it is used by experienced teachers, because it is more likely to teach students how to fill in someone else's blanks than it is to make good decisions as a writer. For this reason, we generally discourage tutors from employing framed paragraphs and steer them toward instructional approaches like the ones described in this chapter that model various ways of organizing writing and help students to "try on" those ways of thinking.

Strategies for Developing Ideas with Details

The difference between a successful piece of writing and an unsuccessful one is often the degree to which ideas in the former are developed with specific supporting details. Ineffective student writing is often very condensed, almost telegraphic in nature. Sometimes, though not as frequently, poor adolescent writers include too many details, failing to make clear which ones are important. Whether they fit either of these profiles, students need to learn to think like their readers, anticipating the quantity and quality of information their audience will need in order to follow an argument or make sense of a story.

How can you help your tutee acquire this sort of understanding? The best way, as is often the case with tutoring, is to model it through a think-aloud, explaining your own thought processes as you write. Make it clear as you talk which of your sentences contains the gist of the idea and which include details to back up your points, create an image, or connect with the reader. You may even want to use two different colored highlighters to offset sentences that express your key ideas from those that provide supporting details.

Other ways to help students develop their writing with details include the following:

- Read samples together of published writing or good student writing in the genre on which your tutee is working. As you read, identify main ideas and supporting details with marginal notes or different-colored highlighters and talk about what kinds of models these texts can provide for his writing. What can he "borrow" from them? See Figure 8.4 for an example of a tutor's think-aloud on how author Jerry Stanley used direct quotations from interviewees in his award-winning book about the Great Depression, *Children of the Dust Bowl* (1992).

- Introduce your tutee to the idea of the Stranger, Ardith Cole's (2002) term for an imaginary person who will read his writing without much background knowledge and for whom he must make it explicit. Show him how to replace vague pronouns with nouns and how to reread to be sure he has answered the Five W's (who, what, where, when, and why). Teach him, as Cole suggests, to make sure that someone reading his text would not need to see the question or assignment to understand the piece.

- Read your tutee's draft honestly, as an interested reader, making marginal notes of places where you need more information to understand it. You and your tutee might even devise a special symbol to indicate that supporting details are needed in a particular place. Eventually, invite him to reread his own work with this lens as a focus, paying attention only to places where he could add detail and ignoring other kinds of errors until he makes another pass through the draft.

- After your tutee has completed a sketchy preliminary draft, ask him to tell you everything he knows about the topic and serve as his scribe as he talks (some adolescents are hampered in their brainstorming process by their awkward handwriting or slow spelling). Return the list of ideas to him and ask him to circle any that are relevant to his piece but have not been included in the draft thus far. Reread the draft together and star where those details could be included.

It is possible that your tutee may struggle to develop his writing with details because he does not yet possess the depth of content knowledge he needs for the

Georgia has been tutoring David, an eighth grader, for about 2 months now. In their last session, David told her that his social studies teacher asked the class to interview someone in their family or neighborhood who had lived through World War II and to write a report about that person's life, based on the interview. David confided that he was struggling with the writing—a fact that Georgia confirmed when she read through his short, and uninspiring, draft. For this reason, she has planned a lesson for today's tutoring session that will help him include details in his report from the interview with his great-uncle, which he really enjoyed.

GEORGIA: David, I know you've been having a hard time making the writing in your oral history report sound very interesting. I was reading through a few books in the school library last week, and I found one where the author does a really good job of including quotes from the people he interviewed. I thought it might help you if we took a look at it.

DAVID: That sounds like a good idea. My report is pretty boring right now.

GEORGIA: It won't be when we're done, I promise. Do you have your notes from the interview?

DAVID: Yeah, they're in my notebook.

GEORGIA: OK, then. Here's what we're going to do. I'm going to read you a little bit from this book, *Children of the Dust Bowl*. It's about a special school for migrant workers' kids in California during the Great Depression. What do you remember about the Great Depression from social studies?

DAVID: Not that much—just that everybody was poor then, and crops failed, and people were jumping off buildings after they lost their jobs, and people were moving across the country to try to find new jobs.

GEORGIA: That's not bad! We can work with that. Well, for this book, the author interviewed all these people who lived during that time and went to that special school. He uses quotes from them to make the story of the Depression really vivid and interesting. I'm going to read you a little bit from the book about the dust storms. As I'm reading, I'll stop every once in a while and talk out loud about what I think the author's doing as a writer with those quotes. Then we can look at your interview notes and see if you can use your quotes in some of the same ways.

I'm going to start right here. (*She points to the page and turns the book so David can see it as she reads.*) *Every morning the house had to be cleaned.* So, the first sentence of the paragraph isn't a quote. I think he's making it clear what the topic of the paragraph is before he uses something he learned in an interview. *Everett Buckland of Waynocka said, "If you didn't sweep the dust out right quick between the storms, you'd end up scooping it out with a shovel."* Ah, here he's introducing a person. He interviewed a lot of different people for this book, so he usually says where they were from to help us readers keep them straight. You probably won't have to do that, or at least you'll only have to do it once, because your paper's going to be about your great-uncle and no one else. He picked a vivid quote from this person, though. It's short, which is good, but I can really picture what would happen if you didn't get after the dust quickly. *And every morning someone had to go check on the animals. The fierce gales buried chickens, pigs, dogs, and occasionally cattle. Children were assigned the task of cleaning the nostrils of cows two or three times a day.* Here he's not using a direct quotation, but it's pretty specific information. I bet he knows that because people told it to him in the interview. Because more than one person likely told him, though, he's not telling you who said it or using quotation marks. Let's go on to the next page, and I'll talk you through a little bit more of it. . . .

FIGURE 8.4. A tutor's think-aloud on using published writing as a model for student writing. Quoted material (in italic) from Stanley (1992, p. 7).

task. If this is the case, the most effective approach may be to read an additional text, view a video clip, or explore a website together, before working directly on the piece of writing. Your conferences with him and observations of him at work should give you a sense of whether his problems are related to a need for more background knowledge.

Strategies for Teaching Surface Features

Like others in the field of literacy, we use the term *surface features* to refer to such aspects of writing as grammar and usage (and, for many people, spelling, though we've chosen to deal with that aspect of writing in Chapter 9). This term differentiates these aspects of writing, also referred to as the *conventions* of writing, from deep structure—that is, the organization and content of a particular text. Since writing is often judged on the basis of its correctness, not just its content, we see it as important for students to learn to use conventions of standard written English. We do not, however, believe that this is where writing instruction should start. So much emphasis has been placed on surface features in some schools that many adolescents—and, sadly, many adults, too—have come to believe that they are poor writers simply because they struggle with something like punctuation. Sometimes, this self-assessment becomes a self-fulfilling prophecy; there is ample evidence to suggest that the overall quality of students' writing suffers when students are too concerned with correctness as they draft (Shaughnessy, 1977). In your tutoring sessions, you will want to place correctness in its proper place, helping students to strive for it without placing it front and center until the bulk of their ideas are on paper.

Your student may not be the only one with concerns about grammar or mechanics, however. If you, too, doubt your command of the surface features of writing, you may feel more comfortable as a tutor if you obtain any of the following user-friendly guides:

> *Sin and Syntax: How to Craft Wickedly Effective Prose* (Hale, 1999)
> *The Elements of Style* (Strunk & White, 2000)
> *Sleeping Dogs Don't Lay: Practical Advice for the Grammatically Challenged* (Lederer & Dowis, 2001)
> *The New Well-Tempered Sentence: A Punctuation Handbook for the Innocent, the Eager, and the Doomed* (Gordon, 1993).

You might choose to read one or two of these books completely before beginning to tutor, or you could simply refer to them on an as-needed basis.

You may also want to browse some of the sites on grammar available on the Web, including the following recommended by Allen (2000):

> Guide to Grammar and Writing (*www.ccc.commnet.edu/grammar/*)
> Grammar Bytes (*www.chompchomp.com*)
> Sue Palmer's Language LIVE (*www.nuff.ox.ac.uk/users/martin/ languagelive.htm*)

Sites such as these are often set up in easy-to-navigate formats that allow you to resolve picky, nagging questions such as when to use *that* and when to use *which*. Some suggest activities for learning particular content that can be adapted for work with your tutee. You may even want to go online together and explore the sites' features, so that your student will be familiar with them and therefore more likely to use them as resources on her own.

In addition to introducing your tutee to these reference guides, you can help her gain greater control over surface features by planning lessons that teach her to deal with the sorts of errors she typically makes. The more authentically these lessons serve the student's own writing, the better off you both will be. As Christenbury (2000) points out:

> Memorizing the usage handbook's definitions, making lists, identifying items on tests, rewriting or identifying someone else's usage mistakes are contextless acts that rarely relate to real students' problems and questions in their own writing. . . . They may lull us into thinking that we are being conscientious teachers, but the fact is these kinds of isolated activities just do not do what we want—which is to improve student writing. (p. 236)

In order to plan responsive lessons around surface features, you will need to examine your tutee's writing closely ahead of time. We recommend obtaining multiple samples, perhaps from her classroom teachers, because she may make different kinds of errors in a lab report than she does in a personal narrative about familiar experiences. As you read, make notes in the margin or on a Post-It about the kinds of errors you see; classifying them will be more important than correcting them, because you'll need a sense of her typical patterns to plan for any of the following activities:

- Mark the lines where errors occur with checkmarks and invite your tutee to revisit those areas to see if she can identify the problem and correct it independently. Your checkmarks will cue her to the specific places in the piece where she needs to attend, which will provide some support without simply telling her the answers yourself.

- Gather at least three examples of the same type of error (e.g., run-on sentences, sentence fragments, lack of subject–pronoun agreement) from your tutee's writing. Tell her that each sentence contains the same kind of error, and invite her to talk with you about what she notices. Help her to develop a generalization in her own words about what is wrong with each of the sentences, then help her to correct those sentences. Keep the generalizations and corrected sentences in a folder or small notebook so she can refer back to them as needed.

- Select a punctuation error that your student commonly makes and find a rule or guideline related to it in a grammar and usage handbook. Invite your student to write some sentences that reflect this rule, using material from her own life. Encourage her to make these sentences funny or ironic; the opportunity to play with language is part of what makes this activity more than just an exercise.

Here's a rule and a tongue-in-cheek sample sentence from Gordon's (1993) handbook: "A comma comes between two independent clauses joined by coordinating or correlative conjunctions, such as *and, but, nor, neither, yet, for,* or *so*. Example: 'You crossed my mind, but you didn't stay there' " (p. 24).

DEALING WITH THE WRITING DEMANDS OF TESTING GENRES

Many of you will be assigned to tutees who have performed poorly on some kind of state examination or whose teachers fear they will perform poorly in the future. One-on-one tutoring with a caring adult is among the best ways to boost students' performance on literacy-related measures that often carry considerable weight and affect the quality of their future opportunities. As long as test preparation does not dominate your sessions to the detriment of other reading and writing activities, we see it as valid, important work for you to do.

Students will do better with test preparation if they approach testing as its own genre—that is, as a type of reading and writing with its own set of rules and structures. According to literacy professors Irene Fountas and Gay Su Pinnell (2001):

> Just as you teach students to read and understand biography or fantasy, you can teach them to read and respond to the genre of tests. Testing reflects a kind of reading and writing that is similar to the reading and writing that people do for authentic purposes. The major difference is that on tests readers are concerned with what the tester is looking for and about displaying their knowledge in a way that shows their competence. (pp. 463–464)

As literacy specialist Ardith Davis Cole (2002) writes in her book about healthy, principled test preparation, students need to learn to make their written performance in these high-stakes situations "look good and sound smart."

One of the best ways to prepare yourself to help students deal with this kind of writing is to examine the tasks the tests require. In New York, where we work, sample test items for examinations in multiple content areas are available on the State Education Department website (*www.emsc.nysed.gov/ciai*). Most states have instituted some kind of testing for students, and good writing skills are often now required for success in content areas such as math, science, and social studies that might not have emphasized literacy when you were in school. We encourage you to browse your state education department's website or published materials to get a sense of what students in your region are asked to do. We expect you'll find that most tasks requiring extended responses in writing have some common features with the following principles and examples we've gleaned from tests taken by middle and high school students in New York:

- *The tests set a purpose for the writing, often asking students to take on a persona and write for another person or group.* The 2002 English examination in New York required high school juniors to construct an essay about historical events that changed the environment for a hypothetical school library exhibit recognizing National Environmental Awareness Month.

- *They require the writer to make a coherent argument and to back up that argument with relevant supporting details.* The 1999 examination in global studies asked students to compare the basic beliefs of two major religions and to "explain how members of the religion, at a specific time and place, acted to unify society or to cause conflict in society."
- *They value writing that has a clear organizational structure.* Sample materials for the 2001 social studies test for eighth graders instructed students to write a "well-organized essay" on causes and consequences of westward expansion in the United States that included an introduction, several paragraphs explaining their position, and a conclusion.
- *They require the writer to edit his or her writing to correctness.* High school juniors taking the 2002 English examination are reminded in the task description to "follow the conventions of standard written English," with one of the five criteria on the scoring guide addressing "the extent to which the response exhibits conventional spelling, punctuation, paragraphing, capitalization, grammar, and usage."

Although general principles of good writing should help students perform on examinations, just as they do in other situations, it can be helpful to introduce students to some high-utility test-taking strategies. Fountas and Pinnell (2001, p. 470) provide the following tips to help students do their best on test questions that require extended written responses. Each of the steps can be modeled and discussed during tutoring sessions.

1. Read and be clear about the question.
2. Note important ideas, phrases, and words as you read the question and any passage provided.
3. Reread to highlight and add to your notes.
4. Organize your notes by numbering, so that they can serve as an outline for your response.
5. Write your response.
6. Reread for sense and completion.

Familiarity with this sequence of strategies should help students do better on examinations. Furthermore, these strategies should also be useful for the times in their lives beyond school when they are asked to write on demand.

CONCLUDING THOUGHTS

We realize that the prospect of teaching writing can be a little intimidating. Many of the tutors we know consider themselves to be better readers than they are writers—a view that affects their confidence when it comes to tutoring writing. This may be the case for you. Do remember, though, that you have had more experience with academic writing than your tutee has. No one expects you to know everything there is to know about writing or writing instruction, and your tutee does have other people—family, classroom teachers, even friends—who are also helping him to develop greater communicative competence. Your work can make a difference, but you aren't the only one engaged in this task. If you approach writing lessons as a problem solver drawing on data from your observations of your student's work, we're sure you will begin to see concrete evidence of improvement . . . and so will your tutee.

CHAPTER 9

Tutoring Sessions
on Word Study and Fluency

Art education student Susan Kral often scoured the Internet for materials and activities she could use with Jalen, her tutee. During one of these Web searches, Sue found a reference to an article titled "Lessons in the Teaching of Vocabulary from September 11 and Harry Potter" (Nilsen & Nilsen, 2002) that described an approach to vocabulary learning that she thought would interest Jalen, who was a fan of J. K. Rowling's fantasy novels. In the article, Nilsen and Nilsen recommend using words from Rowling's stories to teach students how to connect their knowledge of known words to new ones. After reading it, Sue planned a lesson that asked Jalen to decipher meanings for terms such as *omniculars*, *bludger*, and *lumos*, which Rowling had invented using real suffixes, prefixes, and roots. For each word, Sue asked Jalen to think about other words she knew that had similar sounds and/or meanings (e.g., *binoculars* and *omniscient* for the target word *omniculars*). In addition to connecting to her student's interests as a reader, Sue's lesson provided her tutee with valuable practice in breaking difficult words up and thinking about the meanings of those parts relative to her prior knowledge—skills used frequently by proficient readers.

As we suggested in the preceding chapters, *comprehension* and *communicating in writing* are at the heart of literacy development. As such, they should also be at the heart of your tutoring. Some of the most interesting and literate people we know are those who know a lot about words and have strategies for figuring out new ones. Think about it: Words can be fun! Remember your feelings as a young child when you first learned to read a word such as *purple*. Consider what you feel like now, knowing that you have the skills to pronounce a difficult word such as *supercilious*—even though you may still have to scramble to remember its meaning. Remember your delight at realizing that *demote*, *remote*, *promote*, and *emote* are related to one another, sharing a similar root, origin, and meaning! It's easy to get excited about words and their origins, especially when our ever-growing learning about them enables us to sprinkle them purposefully and descriptively throughout our spoken and written language. (We think one of the reasons the Harry Potter books have been so popular is because they do play with language, which readers enjoy.)

English, the primary language of school and business in the United States, isn't always so pleasant for people to learn. The language has a complicated history, drawing on bits of dialect and borrowing words from cultures all over the world. The amalgam can make the language extremely interesting and expressive, but its many sources and often unpredictable patterns can also make it difficult to learn. For this reason, enthusiasm for language study is something you should try to model for your tutee and cultivate in him. Your sessions together will offer you numerous opportunities to help him learn all he can about English words and how they work in reading and writing. Lessons such as the one Sue planned with the Harry Potter novels can make this process seem less intimidating for struggling readers and writers.

Language-rich but "kid-friendly" texts such as J. K. Rowling's novels can also be valuable to you and your tutee because they help support the development of fluency, a term defined by reading researcher Kylene Beers (2003) as "the ability to read smoothly and easily at a good pace, with good phrasing and expression" (p. 205). Your tutee may indeed be a teen who still struggles to read with fluency. You'll be able to discern this difficulty if he mispronounces numerous words, reads very slowly in a word-by-word fashion, or ignores important signals such as punctuation. At a minimum, mistakes like these can be embarrassing to older youth, especially if they are asked to read orally in a public setting like a classroom. A significant number of errors, however, can make a text seem virtually incomprehensible. For this reason, fluency development should be among your primary goals for your tutoring, if it appears that your student needs that kind of support.

In this chapter, we deal with such aspects of word study as word recognition, vocabulary, and spelling. We define what we mean by each of those terms and suggest a number of tutoring approaches to help your student in each of these areas. We show how you can help your tutee put knowledge about the various aspects of word study together in order to read fluently. We recommend some activities that will enhance your student's accuracy, pacing, and expression as a reader. The chapter concludes with a few words about why students who have experienced significant struggles with reading and writing may see these areas of focus as particularly welcome.

WHAT DO WE MEAN BY *WORD STUDY?*

Most youths know the sounds that individual letters make in English and most know a good number of common words on sight. For some teenagers, however, knowledge of words is limited to a smattering of insights about pronunciation and meaning. These individuals are typically thought to lack the phonological ability to match letters and sounds in a way that helps them to access the underlying sound structure of words (Shaywitz, 2003). Students who are learning English as a second or third language often have knowledge of how to figure out words in some contexts but have not yet solved enough English-language mysteries to be able to read English fluently. Individuals in both groups will benefit most from a very specific, systematic plan for intervention developed by such individuals as school psychologists, special education teachers, speech pathologists, literacy specialists, and teachers of new English learners. Do be certain you seek advice from such individuals if you are assigned to a tutee in this group.

You are more likely to find yourself working with a teenager who demonstrates more subtle inefficiencies when it comes to determining the pronunciation, meaning, or spelling of unknown words, and for whom no detailed intervention plan exists. Teens can lack such knowledge if they haven't read enough to infer these strategies, or if no one has cued them to the behaviors of proficient readers. Most adolescents are well served by learning explicit strategies to discern pronunciation or meanings as they read or to select words that make their writing more interesting or precise.

We do not mean that you should spend a majority of your tutoring time teaching letters and what they sound like, or focusing on spelling. Instead, word study needs to be brief. As Sue demonstrated with the Harry Potter words in the preceding section, unless you are privy to an intervention plan, the word study you provide as a volunteer tutor should be tied to the reading or writing you are working on, or to words you or your tutee bring to your sessions because of connections to your tutee's interests. Depending on your tutee's needs, word study involves learning about words and how they work, including generalizations about pronunciation, spelling, and meaning. It also includes finding out how these three aspects of words are connected to one another through their origins, as is indicated in the sections that follow.

WORD RECOGNITION

Word recognition—that is, determining the way a word is pronounced—is central to reading fluency. Although knowing the pronunciation of a word is not always essential to comprehension, those who read more fluently are usually better comprehenders. Think of it this way: Fluent readers can devote more mental energy to understanding what they've read because they don't have to expend as much energy figuring out what individual words mean. That's why it's important to spend some time on word recognition if your student needs help in this area— because it is likely to have a payoff in terms of her comprehension and engagement with reading. You can determine whether or not your tutee needs such support by asking her to read aloud, and by noting errors and looking for patterns in the errors, as we discussed in Chapter 4. If you ascertain that your student needs help with word recognition, some of the following activities should be helpful to her.

Letters and Sounds

By the time they reach adolescence, most young people have acquired a good facility with basic decoding, though many may still struggle to read multisyllabic words (Schoenbach et al., 1999). In rare circumstances, however, you may find an adolescent who does not know all the sounds associated with letters. If this is the case, you will want to review the letters your learner does not know, asking her to write each on an index card or in a notebook. Help your tutee to list a number of words that begin with, end, or contain the letter as examples on the same card, and then invite her to pick one—preferably a word she has already memorized—to serve as a key word to help her remember the letter and its sound. If your tutee struggles with a number of letters, you may decide to review the entire alphabet. Review the troublesome letters for a few moments during each tutoring session, until your student can recognize them automatically.

High-Frequency Words and Sight Words

We read efficiently when we can pronounce most words as whole words, automatically, without having to sound out every letter. The number of words we can recognize automatically increases as we develop more experience with reading. As a proficient adult reader, you likely had to sound out very few, if any, of the words in the preceding sentence.

When adolescent readers struggle, it can be helpful to encourage them to memorize how to read some *sight words* (i.e., those that must be learned by sight because irregularities in their spellings make them difficult to sound out) and some *high-frequency words* (i.e., those that appear so often in printed text that it would be a waste of time to decode them each time they're encountered). The word *write*, for example, is a sight word because the *wr-* combination at the beginning of the word makes it difficult to sound out. It is also a high-frequency word; linguists include it on a list of the 100 most common words in the English language (Fry, Kress, & Fountoukidis, 1993). Teachers who helped to match you with your assigned learner may be able to share a published list of common sight words, such as Fry's List of Instant Words (Fry et al., 1993).

Although these lists can be helpful, there are numerous other ways to select key words for your tutee to learn by sight. For example, you might invite your tutee to pick out two or three words he wants to remember from a text that he just finished reading—a method that offers him choice, an important and motivating factor. You might share your observational notes with him after listening to him read and suggest that he learn the two or three words that stumped him most often. You might select content-area vocabulary that will be useful for understanding a reading selection's central concepts—for example, *revolution*, if you're reading a textbook series about the late 18th century in the United States, or *mitosis*, if you're reading an article about cell biology. Scanning newspaper headlines together and discussing them can suggest sight words with an obvious real-world application. You might even ask your tutee to be on the lookout for interesting or provocative words he encounters outside of your tutoring sessions, including those tied to hobbies or nonacademic interests.

Regardless of how words are chosen, it's helpful to use a similar procedure to learn them. We recommend spending a moment or two practicing the pronunciation of each word—sounding out each syllable separately if it's multisyllabic and noting any patterns that help you personally with pronunciation. (You'll want to model your own word-recognition strategies for your student, just as you modeled your approaches to comprehension and composition.) As with words encountered during all word study, invite him to write the word on a list in a special section of a notebook or on an index card, again jotting clues to pronunciation, definition, and usage, perhaps asking him to write an example of the word in a sentence or to draw an illustration. Review these sight words, too, for a couple of minutes during each tutoring session, until your student is reading them comfortably.

Word Patterns and Syllable Types

Some students will be able to determine pronunciation of an unknown word by zeroing in on a part of the word that they do know, such as a prefix or a suffix. Other learners will need help in breaking longer words into manageable parts, as was the case with Sue Kral's tutee, whom we described at the beginning of this chapter. Do encourage your tutee to preview her reading in advance, scanning for difficult words and trying to discern their pronunciation prior to reading. This conversation, like Sue's lesson, is also likely to help your tutee consider the meaning of these words—an issue we discuss in the next section, focused on vocabulary.

Vast amounts of practice dividing words into precise syllables have not been shown to help readers learn to sound out words. However, a general strategy for breaking a word into manageable segments can be useful. Work with your learner to place a dot under each vowel (*a, e, i, o, u,* and sometimes *y*). Look at the letters that cluster around each vowel to guess at syllables (a syllable, by definition, has at least one vowel), and try, together, to decode by analogy—in other words, to think of other known words that contain syllables that follow the same pattern. Guess the pronunciation from these patterns (Gaskins, Gaskins, & Gaskins, 1991).

Kathy has observed tutors having considerable success in teaching adolescents to categorize syllables by syllable type. Borrowing from Blachman and her colleagues (Blachman, Tangel, Ball, Black, & McGraw, 1999) and Moats (2001), Moore and Hinchman (2002) described six different types of syllables, which you can find listed in Figure 9.1, along with examples of words that fit each type. Tutors who wish to focus on such instruction should spend small portions of a tutoring session, or two, reviewing single and two-syllable words known to your tutee that fit each type, talking about the word patterns apparent for each type and celebrating your tutee's existing knowledge of words and word patterns. Post a chart with each syllable type as a heading—the inside of a file folder works well for this in a two-person tutorial—and begin to categorize syllable types in words you and your tutee find while previewing each reading selection. Begin each word-study segment of your tutorial by reading words you have discerned, to date, and both you and your tutee will quickly begin to feel a sense of accomplishment.

1. closed (e.g., consonant–vowel–consonant)	hat	mop	statistic
2. final *e* (e.g., consonant–vowel–consonant–silent *e*)	make	like	de*vote*
3. open (e.g., consonant–vowel)	my	I	*remote*
4. vowel teams	team	rain	eight
5. vowel + *r* syllables	burn	cart	re*start*
6. consonant + *le*	ca*ble*	bi*ble*	star*tle*

FIGURE 9.1. Syllable types with example words.

VOCABULARY DEVELOPMENT

According to literacy educators Randall Ryder and Michael Graves (1998), teachers can promote students' vocabulary development by (1) teaching specific words, (2) preparing students to learn words independently, and (3) promoting word consciousness—a term they define as "a disposition to notice words, to value them, and use them in precise and effective ways" (p. 32). We see these three roles as being just useful for tutors as they are for teachers, and we suggest that you attend to all three in planning your lessons.

Vocabulary instruction in secondary schools has traditionally focused most on the first goal of teaching specific words. Although this is certainly important, too much attention to it (with too little to the other two) produces students who can call up the meanings of a small body of words they have been formally taught but who are ill-equipped to deal with unfamiliar words they encounter in the reading they do on their own. Focusing on specific words can also foster an attitude in students that vocabulary learning is something they do for a few years in school, at a teacher's behest, rather than as a lifelong activity that they *choose* to pursue. For these reasons, we urge you to plan activities that will help your student develop vocabulary learning strategies as well as foster her interest in, and enthusiasm for, learning new words. We provide some concrete suggestions of ways to accomplish these goals in the remainder of this section.

Selecting Words to Teach and Learn

When you do decide to teach specific words to your tutee, we hope that you will think carefully about which words you choose. Ryder and Graves (1998, p. 40) provide useful guidance in this regard, suggesting we teach only the specific words that meet the following criteria:

1. Understanding the word is important to understanding the selection in which it appears.
2. Students are unlikely to be able to use context or structural analysis skills to figure the word out on their own (if they can, they should be allowed to use these first).
3. The word is likely to be useful outside of the selection currently being taught; for example, students are likely to come across it in other reading.

One way to help your student become more independent as a vocabulary learner is to collaborate with her in determining which words warrant your attention. Ruddell and Shearer's (2002) research suggests that inviting students to choose vocabulary words that they want to study can help to maintain interest and develop content-area knowledge. They invited students to find one or two words each week that they found interesting or thought they would need for something. Students kept a notebook page with a three-column chart containing the word, where it was found, and a rationale for choosing it. In class, they discussed each word's spelling and meaning, drew graphic organizers to show its relation to other words, and recorded an example of how it was used. At the end of each week, students were asked to spell, write a definition, and write a sentence for each word. If you decide to use such a strategy with your tutee, you will want to keep a list of the words for later discussion or review; as with other word-study projects, a special section of a notebook or index cards can be used for this purpose.

Determining Levels of Word Knowledge

Once you and/or your tutee have chosen some vocabulary words to learn, it can be helpful to determine your student's level of knowledge about each of them. One relatively simple way to do this is to construct what Allen (1999) calls a "How Well Do I Know These Words?" chart and then ask your student to place each of the target words into one or the four categories. Figure 9.2 includes a sample chart with words that might be difficult for an adolescent reading the second chapter of Penny Colman's (1995a) book *Rosie the Riveter: Women Working on the Home Front in World War II*. If your student classified most of these words as ones she didn't know at all or had seen or heard but didn't know meanings for, then you would know to allot more time to their study than you would if she classified most as "I think I know a meaning" or "I do know a meaning." This activity can also help students to internalize a way of thinking about words that can be helpful to them when they read on their own. Once they realize that word knowledge is more complex than "all or nothing," it is easier for them to think through how much time and effort they will need to spend on learning particular words.

Visualizing New Words

We introduced you to the idea of visualization in Chapters 2 and 7, when we talked about the comprehension strategies used by proficient readers. What we didn't talk about in much depth, however, was that visualization can serve as a powerful support for vocabulary learning. Aware that some individuals learn words or root words more easily when they can associate that word with a visual image, Hopkins and Bean (1999) recommended use of the vocabulary square, an approach that helps learners make these associations concrete (see Chapter 10 for more on the usefulness of the vocabulary square for students learning English). To make the graphic organizer for this approach, learners draw a square, then divide it into four boxes. The upper left-hand box is for writing the target word or root. The definition should be written in the lower left-hand corner. The upper

Title: *Rosie the Riveter, Chapter 2*

Directions: First, read the words at the bottom of the page silently. After you read each one, write the words from the bottom of the page in the column that best describes what you know about each one.

Don't know at all	Have seen or heard—don't know a meaning	I think I know a meaning	I know a meaning

shortage	armaments
rationing	war bonds
victory gardens	patriotism
home front	essential
civilian	permeated

FIGURE 9.2. Sample "How Well Do I Know These Words?" chart. Figure from *Words, Words, Words: Teaching Vocabulary in Grades 4–12* by Janes Allen, copyright © 1999, with permission of Stenhouse Publishers.

right-hand corner should contain the personal association, with a visual illustration drawn beneath it. An example of a completed square appears in Figure 9.3.

Constructing Other Graphic Organizers

The word-familiarity chart and Hopkins and Bean's square are not the only useful graphic organizers for supporting vocabulary learning. Charts and diagrams, which we've called *graphic organizers* elsewhere in this text, help students to show relationships among words and ideas. Such visual representations of connections among words parallel the way we learn words: by associating them with other words we know (Blachowicz & Fisher, 1996). These graphic organizers can take a variety of forms to classify examples, reveal variations in meanings, demonstrate relationships among types, lay out sequences, or make comparisons. Figure 9.4 includes two types of graphic organizers. Others can be found in Chapters 7 and 8.

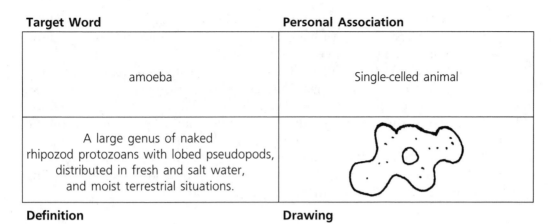

Target Word	Personal Association
amoeba	Single-celled animal
A large genus of naked rhipozod protozoans with lobed pseudopods, distributed in fresh and salt water, and moist terrestrial situations.	

Definition   **Drawing**

FIGURE 9.3. Sample vocabulary square.

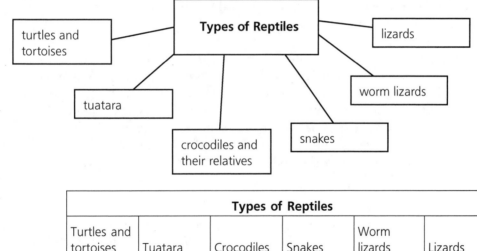

Types of Reptiles					
	Turtles and tortoises	Tuatara	Crocodiles	Snakes	Worm lizards	Lizards
Reproduction						
Body Type						
Habitat						
Food						

FIGURE 9.4. Sample graphic organizers.

When introducing a particular kind of graphic organizer to your tutee, you will want to demonstrate its use with a think-aloud. To maximize this activity, however, be sure to talk with your tutee about the words' relationships, inviting him to fill in some of the blank spaces. You will also want to invite your tutee to generate similar graphic organizers on his own in later tutoring sessions, so that he learns to use them independently as he reads. We think you'll find, as tutor Julie Schopp did with her two learners, that graphic organizers about a few target words can help students make connections to their prior knowledge and future reading. As Julie reflected in writing, "By deciphering [the words with a graphic organizer], the students were able to see how this word applied to the book they were reading and to see how it could be used in the everyday world."

Integrating Multiple Vocabulary Strategies

"Look it up!" is likely to be the teacher-approved answer your tutee will give you when you ask, "What should you do when you come to a word you don't know?" Yet nothing could be further from the actual action most of us take when we find ourselves in this situation. Instead, most good readers use a combination of methods to figure out unknown words—many of which do not require them to get out of their chair! We even decide to skip words that keep us from meeting the purposes we set for our reading. Refer to Figure 9.5 for a list of strategies that you can share with your tutee.

Teach your tutee to check to see if she really needs to know the meaning of the word in question to make sense of the text. You can also teach your tutee to determine meaning from context, by skipping a word and reading segments of text around it. Once your tutee has a general sense of the meaning of a word, use of such *context clues* may be enough to satisfy her need for meaning at the moment.

You can also teach your tutee to guess further about a word's meaning by using *structural analysis*: that is, by looking at prefixes, suffixes, and root words. Ask her if she can think of any words she knows that may be related, structurally, to a word in question (e.g., re*cur*, oc*cur*, *cur*rent; *geo*physically, *geo*graphy). From these related words, she may be able to guess more precise meanings in context.

It may go without saying that textbook glossaries, dictionaries, and notes recorded in class lectures can be used to determine even more precise meanings.

- Use knowledge of letters and sounds to guess at pronunciation and to consider if, once pronounced, it is a word they have heard before.
- Read on to figure out the meaning from the surrounding context.
- Use prefixes, suffixes, and roots to guess meaning and pronunciation.
- Look it up in a dictionary or other reference.
- Decide the word is unimportant and read on.

FIGURE 9.5. Strategies used by proficient readers when encountering unknown words.

This is also a good place to determine, once and for all, the precise meaning of a frequently encountered root word or prefix. However, you should be wary here. You may remember how tedious dictionary exercises can be, even though long "looking up" exercises may develop efficiency with dictionary use. Since all of us are more likely to learn new words through repeated and *varied* exposure, we think it is better to spend a bit of tutoring time on word work, overall, using reference materials only when definitions are necessary for comprehension.

Similarly, when we are writing, we may keep a thesaurus or dictionary at hand—either on our desk or in our computer. Yet most writers draft in a blitz of putting ideas to paper or keyboard; dictionary work while writing can disrupt our fluency to the point of distraction! You will want to explain this aspect of writing to your learner. When he has decided to revise a particular composition, show him how to reread his text to critique repeated word use and vocabulary selection. Then, together, turn to reference materials to find alternative words whose descriptiveness will enhance the quality of his composition.

Developing Word Consciousness

Most of the activities described above have the added benefit of developing awareness of, and interest in, words at the same time they develop strategic behavior and content knowledge. In these cases, word consciousness becomes a fortuitous by-product of other types of vocabulary instruction. There are a few approaches, however, that you can use as a tutor to foster word consciousness deliberately. For example, you and your tutee might keep a vocabulary log or journal in which you both make periodic entries in such categories as "Words that tickle my ear," "Words that make me feel smart," or "Words that make me wonder"—a variation on the word-jar approach described by Allen and Gonzalez (1998). These entries might serve to jog your tutee's memory more if you also include a brief note about where you encountered the words, emphasizing that television shows, movies, and music are legitimate, even recommended, sources of new words to learn and savor. Other quick and low-stress ways to develop word consciousness include the following:

- Make a deal with your student that each of you will come to your tutoring session each week with a "word of the day" to share with one another. Challenge her to stump you with a word you didn't know or to report on a way she was able to work a previous word into casual conversation.
- Set aside some time at the end of your sessions to play board games such as Boggle, Pictionary, and Balderdash, which promote word learning (see Allen, 1999, for a very comprehensive list of other games and the literacy skills they promote).
- Ask your student to write and illustrate an alphabet book on a particular topic of interest that can be shared with younger learners. Finding words for all 26 letters, especially the less frequently used ones such as *x* and *j*, will likely promote some research and thinking. (See Figure 9.6 for alphabet books that we recommend as models for older learners.)

Animalia, by Graeme Base

E is for Empire: A New York State Alphabet, by Ann E. Burg (and other state-related alphabet books published by Gale Group)

H is for Home Run: A Baseball Alphabet, by Brad Herzog (and other sports-related alphabet books by the same author)

Illuminations: A Medieval Alphabet Book, by Jonathan Hunt

The Freshwater Alphabet Book, by Jerry Pallotta (and other science-related alphabet books by the same author)

The Ultimate Alphabet Book, by Mike Wilks

FIGURE 9.6. Alphabet books of interest to older learners.

SPELLING

Examination of your student's writing may suggest that spelling would be a profitable area of study for your tutoring sessions. Don't be shocked if this is the case. Hughes and Searle's (1997) longitudinal study of children as they learned to spell found that even the most able learners in the most supportive literacy classrooms needed considerable time—often more than the 6 years typically allotted for spelling as a separate school subject—to develop into conventional spellers. If this is true for kids who are generally successful at reading and writing, you can easily imagine the spelling needs that might still exist for students who get referred for literacy tutoring.

Faced with evidence that their students need help with spelling, tutors often resort to a traditional approach to instruction that's familiar to them: a list of spelling words on which students are pretested, drilled, and then tested again. We don't recommend this method for classroom teachers, much less for tutors, because it fails to foster much transfer from words spelled correctly on the test to words spelled correctly in students' writing. Nor does it help students to generalize from the small number of words they learn for the test to the many other words that might be related to those words in meaning or sound. Perhaps even more important for your purposes, that method is extremely unlikely to inspire any anticipation on your student's part for your next tutoring session.

Instead, we suggest that you and your tutee pursue activities, such as the following, that will help him adopt new strategic approaches to spelling as well as consider how the spelling system works:

- Teach your student to reread his drafts just for spelling, ignoring other issues in the writing, and circling words he believes are incorrect. This simple first step will help to support his independence as a speller. Even if he doesn't know how to correct the errors yet, it's important for him to learn to isolate them to begin the editing process.
- Make a list together of strategies for figuring out how to spell an unknown word (see Figure 9.7) and show him how to use unfamiliar ones that you think will be useful to him. Demonstrate these in the context of your own

- Look in any book where the word appears.
- Say the word slowly and write down the sounds you hear.
- Figure out how many "chunks" or syllables the word has and make sure they're all in your attempt.
- Make sure each syllable has a vowel.
- Use a word you already know how to spell that has the same sound.
- Write the word several different ways and decide which one looks right.
- Use a mnemonic device (e.g., the principal is your -pal, a friend is a friend to the -end).
- Spell the root word and use those letters in the longer word (e.g., *complete* for *completion*, *invite* for *invitation*).
- Circle or underline the parts of the word you need to check.
- Ask a friend who's a good speller or a teacher for a part of the word—the beginning, so you can find it in the dictionary, or the part of the word that's wrong.
- Look up the word in a dictionary or type it into a computer spell-checker.

FIGURE 9.7. Strategies for figuring out how to spell an unknown word. From *Spelling Inquiry: How One Elementary School Caught the Mnemonic Plague* by Kelly Chandler and the Mapleton Teacher-Research Group, copyright © 1999, with permission of Stenhouse Publishers.

writing or in some shared writing you tackle together. In Figure 9.8, you will find a sample think-aloud used by one tutor as she modeled the use of several spelling strategies for her student while working on a piece of writing together. The "have a go" strategy (writing a word several different ways to see which one looks right) that she showed him is often new and helpful to adolescents.

- Teach patterns, not individual words. Learning word lists is a fairly slow and inefficient way to learn to spell, but an understanding of word *families* (i.e., words that are spelled similarly) can be more generative. Morris (1999) recommends that tutors make up cards for words with common spelling patterns (e.g., *-at, -ake, -ail*) then invite their tutees to sort the cards into categories. As we discussed earlier in this chapter, this approach will also help your tutee with word recognition in reading.
- Teach the four spelling rules that Wilde (1992) says can be applied most consistently:
  1. Use *i* before *e* except after *c*, and in those instances when the vowel combination sounds like "weigh."
  2. Drop *e* before suffixes such as *-ing* (*give* becomes *giving*).
  3. Change *y* to *i* before suffixes such as *-es* (e.g., *puppy* becomes *puppies*).
  4. Double consonants before suffixes such as *-ed* (e.g., *pat* becomes *patted*).
- Show your tutee how to use the computer spell-check function more efficiently by making sure every syllable has a vowel, counting syllables in the target word (e.g., the spell-checker has a harder time generating correct possibilities for a three-syllable word if the writer's attempt only has two sylla-

Luke, a ninth grader, has been asked by his physical education teacher, Mr. Lisi, to complete a short research report on some topic from history related to sports. Because the 2004 Summer Games are going to begin soon in Athens, Luke has chosen to write about the first modern Olympic Games.

Over the past several tutoring sessions, Dylan, Luke's literacy tutor, has been helping Luke consult several websites and nonfiction trade books to do his research. Last week, Luke wrote a rough draft of the two-page paper, with Dylan's help. During today's session, they will focus on editing Dylan's spelling:

DYLAN: OK, Luke, let's take a look at these first couple of paragraphs and see what we need to fix. Does that sound OK to you?

LUKE: Sure, whatever.

Dylan reads the first part of the paragraph aloud to Luke, stopping after the sentence that reads: "The first modern olimpic compatation was held in Athens in 1896."

DYLAN: So, Luke, you've got two spelling errors in this sentence. Do you know what they are?

LUKE: I think they're probably these two. [Luke points to *olimpic* and *compatation*.]

DYLAN: Yup. You got it. What I was thinking I would do is a think aloud for you on how I would fix those two spelling mistakes, if I were writing this piece by myself. That way, I can show you a couple of things you might be able to do on your own when you come to words you don't know how to spell when you're writing by yourself.

Olympic is a pretty hard word, and it's what your English teacher calls a proper noun—one that refers to a very specific thing that needs to be capitalized. Those kinds of words are always hard for me to spell, so I usually like to use a resource beyond my head to help me. I'm thinking I could look up this word in the dictionary—I have a pretty good idea that it starts with *Ol*-, which should make it pretty easy to find. In this case, though, I think I'll just look back at the chapter from that book we read through the other day. I know it's there in the first couple of paragraphs. I'll skim it real quickly. [Dylan shuffles the page a bit.] Ah, there it is: O-L-Y-M-P-I-C. I'm going to capitalize it and change your *i* to a *y*. You were pretty close, except for that. [Dylan crosses out Luke's attempt and writes the correct word underneath it.]

DYLAN: Now I'm going to tackle *compatation*. That's a pretty hard word to spell because it's got a lot of syllables. I think the part that's wrong is the second one. I'm not sure if that *a* should be an *i* or an *e*. They both could make that sound, so I think I'll write it both ways and see which looks better to me. [Dylan writes *compitition* and *competition* on the page next to Luke's attempt.] The second one looks better to me, but I think I'd better check it with another method. Again, I could get the dictionary, and I probably will, just to make sure. One other thing I know to do, though, is to see if I can spell any words that are related to it. That might give me a clue, too. In this case, I know that *compete* and *competition* are related to each other, and *compete* has two *e*'s. That probably means my version with the *e* in it is right. We can check it in the dictionary later.

FIGURE 9.8. Sample think-aloud on spelling strategies.

bles), and trying two different initial letters if the word begins with a sound that can be represented by more than one (e.g., *c* and *k* for /k/; *g* and *j* for /j/).

For more information about teaching spelling to secondary students, you may want to consult an article Kelly published a few years ago (Chandler, 2000) in a periodical for teachers.

WHEN TUTEES STRUGGLE WITH READING FLUENCY

As we discussed briefly in the beginning of this chapter, many teenagers who struggle with literacy appear to lack strategies that will allow them to become active problem solvers when they encounter unknown words or complex meanings, such as those we shared earlier in this chapter and in Chapter 7. Such readers may read in halting, word-by-word fashion or too quickly, with flat intonation and little attention to punctuation or meaning. Such individuals are said to lack reading fluency, and they seem more comfortable with materials whose readability is lower than their current grade placement, even though they show no glaring pattern of word-reading errors.

Reading fluency includes reading speed, rate, and expression—all keys to reading successfully. *Fluency* means being able to read without effort, decoding most words automatically and in meaningful phrases so that comprehension can occur. Three explanations have been offered for dysfluency: slow word recognition, lack of sensitivity to fluency cues that are contained in written language, and failure to connect words and ideas (Meyer & Felton, 1999). As a tutor, you are not likely to be able to ascertain the root cause(s) of your student's lack of fluency. What you can do, however, is to model fluent reading, helping your tutee to learn to read in chunks that sound like meaningful talk, rereading unclear texts and addressing the text's challenges, until understanding is achieved.

Modeling Fluent Reading

Try to be a model for your tutee. Encourage her to talk with you about what she is reading, and let her know that frequent reading experience is likely to be very beneficial for her development of fluency. Because she may not have heard enough fluent reading to understand what she's aiming for, read aloud sections of her texts to provide her with a fluent model and to keep her interest maintained. This may be especially helpful with content-area texts, which can contain a significant amount of unknown conceptual terrain and technical vocabulary words.

Independent Reading of Easy Texts

One of the easiest but often most overlooked ways to promote fluency is to provide students with many opportunities to read easy texts independently. Such reading helps a reader build up exposure to, and thus knowledge of, vocabulary. It can also help a reader acquire a sense of the varieties of sentence structures that can be used in written language. Be sure to tell your tutee about these important benefits to reading frequently.

In Chapters 4 and 6 we talked about how you might determine, often with your tutee's help, what those easy texts might be. Once you've chosen the texts, you may decide to read together, taking turns reading aloud to one another and having fun discussing brief amounts of content. You will also want to encourage your tutee to read segments of text silently—either as you sit nearby to help or at home, marking segments that he likes or has questions about, as was mentioned in Chapter 7.

Do talk with your tutee about this kind of independent reading to gauge comprehension and interest. Such talk will give you insights that will help you select future texts. But remember that the objective here is to increase exposure to written text, not to dissect the text from all possible angles. Discussion of what your tutee found interesting and had questions about can be enough at this point, and then you should move on to selecting another easy-reading text.

Repeated Reading

Repeated reading is also a useful strategy for developing fluency (Samuels, 1979). Using this method, a learner rereads a segment of text aloud repeatedly until fluent reading is achieved. A tutor can orchestrate this exercise by reading the passage to the learner first, once or several times, so that the learner can mimic the tutor's fluency—perhaps during the reading of one of the easy books mentioned in the preceding section. Do use short passages—and short segments of your tutoring session—for this activity. You'll want to limit the time spent on work in this area; the focus of a volunteer's time with older youths should be on reading and comprehension of texts, as needed, for their short- and long-term success.

Be certain to explain why you think repeated reading is a good idea. Have your tutee reread and practice a paragraph or two from selected texts until he can read it with expression, and without hesitation. Talk briefly with your tutee about how reading can be made more fluent as you do this; such talk must be brief and focused, or you will lose your tutee's attention. Follow it with immediate opportunities for your learner to try out the ideas you just presented, giving him a chance to mimic your behaviors in repeated reading.

Help her, too, to understand how we stop and solve problems we encounter when reading—by decoding, looking up definitions of important unknown words, or tracking the wording of a complex sentence. Show her, too, how most of us work on a segment of text at a time, from heading to heading in an expository text, or a paragraph or two at a time in a narrative. Your learner also may need to know how commas and periods provide cues to phrasing. After you've stopped to do this problem solving, resume the rereading, and continue in this manner until comprehension occurs.

Repeated reading can be especially fun if you do it for a real-world purpose, such as rehearsing for a reader's theatre performance or a reading buddy session with younger children (Worthy, Broaddus, & Ivey, 2001). Your host teacher may know of a play that your tutee can perform with other tutees, allowing time for each of them to rehearse fluent reading of their assigned lines. There may also be a nearby elementary or nursery school that you could visit with your tutee so that he can be a reading buddy to another youngster.

Unrehearsed Oral Reading

The previous section included recommendations for instructional approaches to promote fluency. Before we conclude, let us say a few words about an activity that is *not* helpful to dysfluent readers: unrehearsed oral reading (Worthy et al., 2001). Even if you're not familiar with this term (or with a synonym, "round-robin reading"), we're guessing that you've experienced it at some point. The typical scenario goes something like this: A teacher selects a text for the whole class or a small group to read together. Students in the class take turns reading the text aloud, one paragraph each, until the text is finished.

Such reading is likely to occur in classrooms when teachers are concerned that students are not reading assignments, and they wish to cover the terrain in this manner. However, without rehearsal, many students become so concerned with pronouncing words that they are not likely to comprehend the material. This kind of reading is also generally hard to listen to, since some readers are less fluent than others. (Kathy remembers a teacher who used to fall asleep when her class was reading their social studies book in this manner.) Moreover, real-life reading is more likely to demand silent reading of extended text, so that is the skill with which our students need practice.

Tutors can frequently make the same mistake as these classroom teachers, by asking their tutee to read aloud throughout the tutoring session. Without giving the student a chance to rehearse, the pressure here is on performance and not comprehension or fluency. Silent reading is usually better to encourage. Even so, Kathy has known a number of tutees who have begged to read aloud during tutoring. This request might need to be negotiated with your learner, depending on her age and persuasiveness. Even if you do succumb to such requests, try to persuade your learner to spend some time with you and on her own reading silently and explain why this is important.

Prompting

Adolescents who have struggled with reading over a long period often need to be reminded of problem-solving strategies they can use when they read something that they do not understand. Your tutee may even look to you to help her fix her mistakes. Remember that it's better to prompt than it is to correct or fix errors, because prompting allows a learner to problem solve on her own, using strategies that can then become part of her independent reading repertoire. Use the kind of prompts that a learner can make a part of her own problem-solving strategies. Kylene Beers (2003, p. 217), a teacher and researcher who frequently works with struggling readers, suggests using the following prompts when your student gets bogged down in her reading and can't continue, or when she asks for your help:

- "Can you read that again?"
- "Do you see a part of the word you recognize?"
- "What word would make sense here?"
- "Can you divide the word into syllables and sound it out that way?"
- "Can you sound it out slowly and see if that helps?"

CONCLUDING THOUGHTS

Some tutors we've known have shied away from incorporating work on word study and fluency into their sessions, even when their students appeared to need such attention. Often they worried that their students would be bored, or possibly insulted, by lessons that seemed too babyish or too focused on the minutiae of literacy. We don't mean to suggest that these concerns are unwarranted—some adolescents do balk at spending time on decoding lessons or rereading easy texts to develop fluency. Word study can indeed seem tedious and unduly abstract, especially when lessons drag on too long or when tutees have not learned to see such work as valuable.

Sometimes, however, young people embrace these emphases because they know that this instruction will benefit them as readers and writers. For example, Kathy once observed a tutor whose seventh-grade student had difficulty decoding unfamiliar multisyllabic words. The tutor was not convinced that her tutee really needed help with pronouncing such words, even though those who observed their sessions together could see that her tutee had no real strategy for dealing with the long words he hadn't seen before—a pattern that would cause special difficulty as he approached the technical vocabulary of high school subject-area study. The tutor agreed to try a lesson focused on the syllable types discussed earlier in this chapter. As she began to review the six types, her tutee grabbed her by the arm and said, "Yes! This is the stuff I need to understand! No one has explained it to me before."

Planned carefully and sensitively, your tutoring sessions can indeed provide a space and a time for students such as this young man to learn about aspects of literacy that no one else has explained. Teens do like to learn how things work, including strategic ways to approach pronunciation, spelling, word usage, and fluency in their reading and writing. If your student needs help in any or all of these areas, remember to keep your lessons short, focused, and connected to his real-world interests as a reader and writer. Remember, too, that emphasizing comprehension and composing, the focus of Chapters 7 and 8, will likely help to motivate him to learn more about the patterns, nuances, and idiosyncrasies of written language.

PART III

FOLLOW-UP
AND REFLECTION

CHAPTER 10

Dealing with Common Problems

Last fall, Kelly's husband, Jim, began a full-scale remodeling of their second-floor bathroom. Always intrepid with new home-improvement challenges, he bought Sheetrock, a tile cutter, and new fixtures, and then began major demolition. A few months after the job was completed, Kelly and Jim saw a television show on Home and Garden Television (HGTV) devoted to bathroom renovation. Although both were pleased with their finished project, several tips presented on the program would have made the process go more quickly and easily. The show didn't cover everything they needed to know, as no television producer—no matter how experienced—could have predicted what they would encounter behind the plaster walls of an old and very idiosyncratic house. Nonetheless, it could have provided a useful guide to the renovation, had they seen it before the work began.

The same is true for us and your tutoring: We can't predict exactly what will happen to you, because tutoring involves human relationships in a variety of social contexts. Your experience will undoubtedly be unique—different even from peers who tutor in the site. That said, we have seen some patterns in tutors' experiences that are worth sharing here to help you prepare for your work with students. We discuss these problems in this chapter along with some suggestions for potential solutions, so that you, like the homeowners who watch HGTV before tackling a new project, can strategize about how to approach your new task.

The chapter is organized around a series of questions and answers in a few broad categories we see as important. Although the questions don't come verbatim, from real tutors, they're far from hypothetical. Instead, they represent a paraphrasing and, in some cases, a composite, of questions we've been asked over the years by numerous tutors working in a variety of contexts. We hope that this Q & A will help you to anticipate—and possibly ward off—some of the struggles tutors typically face. You may also find yourself revisiting this chapter in the midst of your tutoring if problems arise that you did not expect.

MANAGEMENT AND BEHAVIOR ISSUES

Q: My tutee is absent a lot of the time, which makes it tough to have any continuity in our tutoring sessions. Last week, he was suspended from school for fighting, and I'm not sure when he'll be coming back. What should I do?

A: In our experience, this is not an uncommon problem. Many of the same factors that put kids at risk for literacy failure also contribute to absenteeism and behavior problems: instability at home, skill gaps, poverty, and more. When her students struggle with their tutees' sometimes erratic behavior, Kelly reminds them that the kids who come to school every day with their homework done are usually *not* the ones who need help from a tutoring program in the first place. Consequently, tutors need to acknowledge that such issues come with the job and learn to deal with them as best they can, rather than waste much time or energy lamenting them.

We have two suggestions related to the problem of absenteeism. First, it may be helpful to tutor two students at a time, because one of them may be present even if the other is not. This way, your visit to the site will be less likely to be in vain, even if you don't see both tutees every session. You may want to ask your mentor teacher or tutoring supervisor if there is another child with similar needs to your first tutee who might benefit from joining your tutoring sessions. Second, you may want to use some concrete strategies to reinforce attendance. Although it's unlikely that a tutor could do anything to prevent a behavior-related suspension, you can be deliberate about encouraging your tutee to show up for school, especially on the days you're planning to meet. For example, at the end of each session, you can pique his interest in coming back by previewing attractive aspects of the next one, especially if you give him choices about what he reads or an opportunity to research his interests. If you have contact information for your tutee, you may want to call or e-mail him a day or two before your next session, to remind him you're coming and to say you're looking forward to seeing him. If he is absent, follow up on that issue the next time you see him: Ask him where he was, and tell him you missed him. You may be surprised by how much these simple relationship-building strategies contribute to your tutee's feelings of responsibility to you and your time together.

Q: My tutee's pretty hostile toward me. She resents the fact that she gets pulled out of class for extra help, and she seems determined to sabotage everything I try. Any suggestions?

A: Sometimes young people who struggle with literacy are hostile to their tutors as a "cover" for embarrassment about their poor skills. Many have developed an elaborate set of coping strategies to deal with, and sometimes camouflage, their lack of proficiency with reading and writing, and individual tutoring can threaten to reveal what they've taken great pains to disguise. If you suspect this is the case, we recommend planning some low-risk activities that will allow you to assess your student's skills but that will not put her on the spot. For example, you might ask her to read aloud to you from a book of her choice, rather than one she's never seen before. In addition, you will want to attend to relationship building as explicitly as literacy development. Be sure to plan for time to talk informally about both of your lives and interests, not just skills and strategies, and perhaps the hostility will fade.

Here's something else to think about: Pull-out tutorials can sometimes create resentment on the tutee's part if she feels like she is missing important or interesting class activities. This is especially true if her attendance at your sessions puts her behind in assignments for which she is being graded. You should ask your student about how her absences are being handled by her teacher. If, for example, she ends up with double homework—the regular assignment, plus any missed classwork—on the days she works with you, you might tactfully ask her teacher about adjusting the classwork expectations on those days. Such an adaptation may help to keep your tutee from viewing, quite logically, your literacy intervention efforts as detrimental to her overall success as a student.

Q: My tutee is really disruptive. It's very hard to get him to focus, and he often disturbs other tutor–tutee pairs. What can I do about this?

A: Our first piece of advice is to be straight with your tutee about his behavior. Although we don't recommend nagging or scolding a disruptive student (this will probably make him more hostile or defensive), it may be helpful to say, in as neutral a tone as possible, something like the following: "The last couple of times we've met, it seems like it's been hard for you to stay focused. What's going on with that, and is there any way I can help you be more productive?" Another strategy might be to move to another location for your tutoring. Sometimes students are more disruptive when they have a peer audience for their behavior—especially if that audience will be amused by your struggles to keep the session moving. Although we don't recommend tutoring in a private space for the reasons outlined in Chapter 3, you might find a corner of the library or the community center where staff are present but where other students, especially those who might tempt your tutee to misbehave, are less likely to be. If your tutee's behavior is related to a desire to "cover" for his poor skills, such a move may be especially beneficial.

You may also want to think about addressing these issues in your lesson planning. For example, it may help your student to stay on track if you break your session plan into smaller, more manageable chunks, especially at the beginning of your time together, and work toward more sustained activities over time. Changing activities as the session progresses can help to keep your student's interest and engagement high. You may want to build more choice into the agenda, in relation to writing topic, order of activities, or texts to be read. Some learners simply want to feel like they have more control over their actions than what a tightly planned tutoring session can allow. You might also think about building in some literacy-focused rewards at the end of the session—the chance to read a favorite magazine, look something up online, or check his e-mail—if your tutee shows improvement in his focus. Whatever you decide, we recommend touching base with a teacher or staff member who knows your tutee. If he is disrupting your tutoring sessions, chances are high that he is disruptive in other settings as well, so others who work with him may have suggestions for strategies you can adopt.

COMMUNICATION WITH TEACHERS AND STAFF MEMBERS

Q: My tutee doesn't seem like she needs tutoring. When I ask her to read out loud, she makes almost no mistakes. I don't see why she was chosen for extra help. What would you do?

A: In this situation, we first suggest making contact with the teacher or staff member, if that's possible, and asking that person directly why the student was referred and what he or she would like you to work on together. Unless it is very early in the school year or program, that person will know more about the student than you will, and he or she can help you target areas of need that might not be obvious from one or two oral reading sessions.

Just because your tutee demonstrates error-free oral reading doesn't mean she needs no help, however. Some students are able to read the words on a page without necessarily constructing meaning from them. You may want to review the strategies presented in Chapter 4 for assessing her comprehension. If you do discover that your student is a generally fluent reader with good comprehension and you don't receive more specific instructions from a teacher or program supervisors, then you may want to try one or both of the following:

1. Increase the amount of nonfiction you read together. Many adolescents have a good deal more experience reading fiction than they do expository texts. For this reason, nonfiction can be more challenging for them, and it also increases their vocabulary and content knowledge, which is always good.
2. Focus more on writing than reading. Often, students who are fairly competent readers still struggle to develop their ideas in sophisticated ways with supporting details. You will still want to do some reading together, however, to model specific aspects of good writing that those texts demonstrate.

It's worth noting that both of these approaches may position your student to do better in standardized testing situations, because these tests often include a high percentage of nonfiction passages and require students to develop their ideas with details in writing.

Q: No one ever seems to have time to talk to me about my tutee. I know I'm supposed to connect my work with him to his classroom program, but that's hard to do without more information.

A: As we discussed in Chapter 3, classroom teachers and staff members for community organizations juggle multiple responsibilities, only one of which is maintaining contact with tutors who may enter their site once or twice a week. Finding time to talk with them about your tutee's needs can indeed be a challenge. In addition to connecting with each other outside of class via telephone or e-mail, you might find it helpful to communicate through occasional notes or, more formally, a dialogue journal kept on-site, to which both of you contribute. We think you'll have more success if you ask a teacher or staff member to respond to specific questions rather than to talk to you in a general way. For example, you might write a note such as this one:

> "I'm noticing in our tutoring sessions that DeShaun doesn't seem to keep track of what he comprehends as he reads aloud. I think he may see reading as just pronouncing the words, not necessarily understanding them. Do you have any suggestions for how I might work on this area with him? Are you doing anything related to comprehension that you would like me to reinforce?"

You might come by the school or the center to pick up the person's response a day or so before your next session, so you can use the information to plan with, or you could even provide the teacher with a self-addressed stamped envelope to mail it back to you—a convenience that would surely be appreciated.

If your tutoring program doesn't formally require you to spend some time in your tutee's classroom, you might schedule a time with his teacher to visit and learn more about the curriculum. While you're there, you could peruse your student's textbook, read through folders of completed work if the teacher maintains them, and take notes about any assignments or information posted publicly in the room. This experience may provide you with useful information about the classroom program, even if it's difficult for you and the teacher to find one-on-one time to meet.

Q: My tutee's teacher keeps giving me work to do from her science class. It's hard to work on literacy skills and strategies when we need to do questions at the end of the textbook chapter, and I worry that we never get to work on anything my student is interested in. What should I do?

A: Given how jam-packed most school curricula are today, we can understand why a teacher might want you to support the classroom program. At the same time, tutoring that focuses exclusively on homework help is less likely to move struggling students forward than tutoring that focuses on developing their reading and writing skills. Sometimes these aren't mutually exclusive goals, however. When asked by a teacher to complete the reading of a required textbook chapter during a tutoring session, some tutors we know have found it helpful to do so but simultaneously to show their students some strategies for dealing with difficult vocabulary or finding main ideas that can then be applied to *any* text they encounter, not just the required one.

Some tutors take a different approach, using the first few minutes of their sessions to help their tutees get started on homework assignments, then reserving the rest for literacy-related instruction and practice. You might work through the first five items in a 20-question problem set together, asking your tutee to articulate a plan in her own words for completing the remainder of the problems independently. In this way, you provide additional support for your student that increases her chances of successfully completing the homework assignment, but you also reserve a considerable chunk of time for working on the reading and writing skill deficiencies that led to your student's identification for literacy tutoring in the first place.

Q: My tutee completed a quickwrite about taking care of his baby brother that included a report of his frustration and even hitting his brother. It sounded like abuse. Should I tell someone?

A: If you develop good rapport with your tutee, he may tell you, or write about, some of what goes on in his life outside of school. If something he says sounds like a crime is involved (e.g., underaged sex, beating, drug sales) or as though someone could get hurt (e.g., pregnancy, suicide), you should tell your host or mentor teacher so that reporting and response procedures can be initiated. Schools have systems in place for dealing with such concerns, involving social workers, counselors, and police as needed and as school rules dictate. If you do not report something your tutee tells you in confidence, you can be held liable for the occurrence of criminal acts. Imagine your response if a tutee confessed suicidal impulses, you did not say anything to anyone about it, and your tutee decided to take action.

PLANNING AND INSTRUCTION

Q: My tutee speaks English as a second language, and I'm not sure how to help him, especially since I don't speak his first language. Any suggestions?

A: When preservice English teacher Barbara Schrom tutored two girls who were native speakers of Bosnian, she invited them to make notes for themselves in both Bosnian and English as she explained directions or as they defined vocabulary words together. Later, after the session was concluded and they no longer had Barb or each other for support, the girls could use these notes as a reference. This approach gave them additional practice in writing English, but concepts and ideas were also reinforced by their use of the language in which they were most comfortable. Experts in the field, such as Mora (2001–2002), argue that encouraging second-language learners to use their native language as a strategic learning tool can support their learning of English, not impede it.

We also recommend the use of visual aids to help learners acquire English vocabulary. Liz Paushter, another tutor studying to be a teacher, reported a good deal of success when she and her tutee worked on new words using Hopkins and Bean's (1999) visual-vocabulary square (described in Chapter 7). Liz wrote the following in an online posting to other tutors in her college class:

> "Every week we have been doing vocabulary boxes, from that article we read. . . . Well, today I asked her what the words meant from last week, and she immediately remembered the picture she had drawn and then remembered the definition. It was fantastic. This is a girl who is an ESL student, and she whipped those off better than I could."

In this situation, the additional visual support of the sketch helped to transcend the language barrier and aided Liz's student in making connections between English vocabulary and terms she knew in the native tongue.

Q: My tutee doesn't talk to me. At all. I hear her talking with her friends before we begin our tutoring, but when she's with me, she clams up and responds to all my questions with grunts or one-word answers. Can you suggest some activities to get her to open up?

A: Our first piece of advice on this subject is about how to view this situation, not necessarily what to do about it. We think it's important to realize that tutoring often presents a new and unfamiliar context for students; it's only natural for them to be sizing you up and trying to determine whether you're safe or trustworthy before they open up. Your tutee knows her friends a lot better than she knows you, so it's not surprising that she would be more open with them.

That said, however, there are some strategies you can use to create a more comfortable environment for your work, and one of them might involve reflecting on the questions you ask. Parent guides often advise against subjecting teenagers to a barrage of questions, because young people can sometimes perceive innocent inquiries as grilling. For this reason, you might want to try making some statements about your personal life, interests, or literacy habits, and then wait to see whether your student will respond, rather than immediately putting yourself in the position of the interrogator. When you do ask questions, make sure that it's clear to your tutee that she can ask them of you, too. For example, when Matt Vogt, a student of Kelly's, began tutoring an eighth grader, he administered an interest inventory as part of their first session. For every question Matt asked, Carmelo was able to ask a question of Matt, as long as the questions were appropriate for a school-based relationship. This kind of mutual disclosure set a positive tone for their subsequent interactions and helped Matt develop rapport with his tutee. Be patient; we're guessing this issue will improve over time.

Q: My student is engaged in our tutoring sessions as long as we're reading texts on a subject he likes. Unfortunately, the only subject he likes is hip-hop music. If I try to get him to read something else, he's really uncooperative. Any ideas?

A: If you can't bear the thought of reading another Nelly article from *Teen People* with your tutee, take heart. There are plenty of ways to nudge your student toward greater variety in his reading material. For one, you can introduce new text genres without necessarily changing the topic. Trina Nocerino's tutee, Richard, whom we discussed in Chapter 6, didn't show much interest in reading material about anything other than basketball. Instead of trying to coax him into other areas, Trina assembled a selection of texts on that topic that varied widely in terms of their genre. Over the course of their time together, they read poetry, magazine articles, web sites, and biographies—all of which required different skills and strategies of Richard as a reader. Similarly, a student with a passion for hip-hop might be steered from performer profiles to explore such texts as an online article about an ATM-like device for downloading music (*http://www.howstuffworks.com/musicteller.htm*) or a book for young people, such as *One Nation Under a Groove: Rap Music and Its Roots* (Haskins, 2000).

Although your tutee can certainly learn and refine his skills and strategies while reading a number of texts on the same topic, you may indeed want to stretch his horizons in terms of subject matter, and there are numerous ways to do this. If you asked your student to complete an interest inventory early on in your sessions, you might revisit that document and see if it provides additional clues about possible topics to explore. Ask him to talk to you about television programs or films he's seen and liked. Although exploration of popular culture is often off-limits in class, talk about those interests can often provide ideas for print texts, especially nonfiction ones, to be used in tutoring. For example, an avid fan of the television drama *CSI: Crime Scene Investigation* might be interested in Donna Jackson's book *The Bone Detectives* (1996). You might also want to plan a tutoring session around a text about a passion or hobby of your own, because a tutor's own enthusiasm can sometimes be infectious.

Q: My student's literacy skills are so poor that sometimes I'm not sure if I'm making a difference at all. How can I be sure I'm helping her?

A: Occasionally, volunteer or college tutors are matched with adolescents whose problems with decoding words or writing basic sentences are so severe that they outstrip the expertise the tutors possess. These cases are rare in our experience, but they do occur. If you fear that your student's processing problems are so significant that she is making no progress in your sessions, we urge you to talk to your program director, who may be able to seek additional help or possibly even formal testing from a certified reading professional.

It is more often the case, however, that tutors make a difference but fail to see it, either because the progress comes in the form of what one of our students called "baby steps," or because the progress is revealed in a time or place other than the tutoring sessions. Janet Allen, an expert in the field of adolescent literacy who works frequently with teachers, often talks about the importance of "planting a seed." She explains that many of the things we do to support struggling students' learning don't lead to dramatic, immediate change. This is especially true when tutoring a young person once or twice a week for a year or half a year: Sometimes the seeds you plant don't flower in the time that you're tending the garden! Keep this in mind as you work with your tutee, observe her closely to see slight indicators of improvement, and remember that the social and emotional support you provide as a caring adult may be as significant to her growth as your literacy-focused interventions.

CONCLUDING THOUGHTS

Occasionally, tutors embark on a tutoring relationship with a warning from a teacher or program director about their tutee's poor attitude or negative behavior. Whereas this preview can sometimes hold true, in other cases, the student in question shows his tutor an entirely different side of his personality. Stephanie Fox, a graduate student preparing to be a secondary teacher, experienced this phenomenon while tutoring a sixth grader. She posted the following message to a website for tutors in her program:

"Well, I have finally had my first session in tutoring. I was told by my host teacher that the boy that she was giving me came off as kind of a hard kid. I had noticed this before she told me. This kid acted completely disrespectful in class; as a matter of fact, he has had a different seat every time I see him. In my first session with him we both filled out a 'get to know you' questionnaire. One of the questions was 'What most people don't know about me is . . .' and my tutee answered the question by writing, '. . . that I am nice.' It blew me away; in fact, that was more important and valuable to me than any amount of reading and writing that we did that day!!"

What seems important to us about this anecdote is that Stephanie's one-on-one tutoring relationship allowed her a glimpse of this student that she might not otherwise have seen. Although her tutee had positioned himself as a difficult student in his class—a large class, because it was taught by two instructors—his response to her inventory question helped her to see him in a different way. Perhaps just as significant, she realized that her tutoring sessions could provide him with a space to *be* a different person, to try on a new self who was more engaged and cooperative than usual, because he had a fresh start with her. Her case study paper, reporting on a semester's worth of work with him, depicts her student as an energetic and engaged learner—someone with multiple strengths as well as needs.

We've found Stephanie's experience to be fairly common: Tutors often find that students who behave quite differently in other settings respond very positively to individual attention. We believe the chances that this will happen for you are increased exponentially if you are aware of the challenges that tutors often face and if you take a proactive approach to addressing those challenges. We hope that these scenarios have given you some new insights into the issues as well as suggested various strategies you might try when faced with one of them in your tutoring. The most helpful strategy, however, may simply be to stay in regular communication with those at your site, whether it's a school or community-based organization. Although your tutoring may take place one-on-one with an adolescent, we predict that there will be plenty of other people—fellow tutors, teachers, program directors—who will have suggestions for addressing issues that we, as people who don't know your context, can't even possibly begin to foresee. Don't hesitate to "pick their brains," and remember that you can serve as a resource for them as well in thinking through and brainstorming solutions to the sorts of problems profiled in this chapter.

CHAPTER 11

Reflecting on Your Tutoring Experience

In the fall of 2002, Syracuse University undergraduate Jennifer Pearl signed up for a course that required her to serve as a literacy tutor on a weekly basis. In part because of her major in International Relations, Jen was assigned to work with two students who were learning English as a second language. Aware that Jameel and Naila were originally from Yemen, Jen planned her first tutoring sessions around some reading material about that country. This snippet from a journal entry she wrote about her third lesson demonstrates how useful it can be for tutors to take regular time to document and reflect on their work with students:

> "Well, the first part of the lesson ran long, and we ended up reviewing the strategies from last week the whole time, using the captions for photos of Yemen I downloaded from Encarta and brought the previous week. We read about Yemeni folk dancers and about the skyline in the city of Aden. The first was a bit difficult—I've found context clues can be very misleading. However, Jameel and Naila are doing very well in activating previous knowledge about Yemen to help them decode words in longer passages. I was especially proud when, working off of one another and with a little guidance from me, the two interpreted the meaning of 'mixture.' Jameel identified 'mix' inside of the word, Naila defined 'mix,' and using context clues (the sentence talked about a mixture of old and new structures in Aden), they figured it out."

As you read, you probably noticed that this excerpt from Jen's journal further illustrates some key principles about assessing and evaluating student learning that we laid out in Chapter 4. For example, she used her entry to document concrete and specific data about how her students collaborated with each other and with her to figure out the meaning of a new English word. These data were helpful to her in planning other sessions focused on word study. She also made some notes about the pacing of the lesson that allowed her to make adjustments in how she timed future lessons. For the purposes of this chapter, however, Jen's reflection is important more because of what it allowed her to do when her tutoring concluded than what it allowed her to do in her week-by-week planning. Asked to write a case study report about her students' growth 4 months after she began tutoring them, Jen was able to return to these records and consider patterns over time. From this reflective process, she learned a good deal about her two students that she might not otherwise have known . . . and she learned just as much about herself as a tutor.

Because we have seen similar benefits for many tutors with whom we've worked, we suggest a number of strategies in this chapter that promote reflection on your sessions with your tutee, both at the midpoint and at the conclusion of your tutoring experience. We also make recommendations about how to write a detailed and sensitive case study report, as Jen did, and how to bring closure to your relationship with your tutee when it is time for your sessions to cease. Finally, we urge you to consider the implications of your tutoring experience in light of your future goals and aspirations, whether you are a preservice teacher or a community volunteer.

"BIG PICTURE" REFLECTION

We hope that we've already make a strong case for the value of reflecting on your tutoring from one session to another. In addition, we highly recommend taking stock of the experience with a wider lens, one that allows you to compare various pieces of data to each other and to see patterns over time that you might otherwise miss. You might think about this broader sort of reflection as an aerial view of a big chunk of terrain, with daily or weekly reflection more like the immediate view a traveler sees from the ground. Each perspective offers different information to the tutor, just as it does to the traveler.

One of the easiest ways to reflect on your tutoring over time is simply to reread the complete contents of your tutoring binder, including your plans, materials, and daily reflections. Many tutors find it useful to do this at the midpoint of whatever period they're scheduled to tutor, whether they're signed up for a semester, a summer, or a year-long commitment. It will be just as useful at the end of your service. The procedure is simple: After rereading everything in your binder, take out a blank piece of paper, set a time limit (15 minutes works well), and write without stopping for the duration about your impressions of the material you just read. The simple act of writing generally tends to jump-start reflective processes, helping you to zero in on key themes in your tutoring. If possible, you might want to share your freewrite with another tutor from your site, because talking about your informal writing may help you identify additional patterns and themes.

Another flexible approach to reflection is to browse materials in your tutoring binder and use different-colored Post-It notes to mark information that strikes you as important. You might find it helpful to devise a color-coding system to keep track of different kinds of information (e.g., red flags for evidence of improved engagement with literacy; blue ones to indicate use of a particular strategy, such as questioning or inferring; yellow ones to note increased fluency with oral reading). Such a system allows you to refer back to particular examples easily, and the frequency of the different-colored flags visually reveals the patterns in the data.

Reflecting at the Midpoint

In addition to reflection strategies that can be used at any time, we recommend using some strategies specifically designed to help you reflect on your tutoring after you've been meeting with your student long enough to begin to know her but at a juncture when you still have time to make adjustments in your approach. Partway through your tutoring experience, for instance, you might follow Ruth Hubbard's (1993) recommendation to write a two-column journal entry that looks like this:

Five Things I Know about Shakira	Five Things I Need to Find Out
• She lives with her mom, whom she describes as an avid reader of romances.	• How much she reads at home.
• She likes horror fiction by Stephen King and Dean Koontz.	• What texts she's read in school that she hasn't hated.
• She reads out loud in a really choppy way.	• What she does when she comes to a word she doesn't know while reading.
• She's failing freshman English for the second time.	• How she's doing in her other classes (e.g., biology, consumer math, global studies).
• Her spelling of fairly common words tends to be inconsistent.	• What she knows about using the computer spell-check function.

As Hubbard explains, this method can help to point out "emerging" themes in your understanding of your student as well as "holes" in your data (p. 144). Reflecting on what you need to find out can help you set a broad agenda that might drive your daily planning for the rest of your time together. You might even find it useful to add a third column to your chart with the following heading: "How Can I Find Out These Five Things?"

Another approach to midpoint reflection is to write a stream-of-consciousness narrative *from your tutee's perspective* about such topics as your tutoring sessions, his English class, and his perceptions of himself as a literacy learner. Try to imagine what your tutee's inner voice sounds like and capture that on paper as authentically as possible. Use any phrases that you typically hear him say, and try hard to keep your own point of view from infiltrating your imagined version of his. We suggest writing nonstop for 10–15 minutes because this makes it easier to get "into character," and, of course, censor yourself as little as possible. When participants in Kelly's student-teaching seminar tried this approach while tracking a student of interest to them, some of them discovered new insights about their learners. Others realized they didn't know enough about their students' viewpoints and attitudes to imagine even the beginnings of an inner monologue—a realization that sent them back to their students for formal interviews, written dialogues, and simple conversation in order to learn more about their students' perceptions of themselves and their worlds. Like Hubbard's two-column chart, this informal writing should be seen as an activity with the potential to reveal the limits of what you know about your tutee; it's not meant to "appropriate" your student's voice or to come to definite conclusions about what he might be thinking without asking him. Instead, we view it as one tool among many that can help you consider other perspectives than your own on the tutoring sessions in which you both participate.

Reflecting When Sessions Conclude

Midpoint reflections can help you consider patterns in your tutoring when time remains to make adjustments. You'll also want to engage in activities that allow you to take stock of your experience, with an eye toward improving your future work with other students or simply to understand your time as a tutor in a deeper way. Your student can play a vital role in this process.

Just as some tutors ask their students to complete weekly quickwrites about what stood out for them after each lesson (see Chapter 5), others ask their tutees to complete an informal piece of writing that contains feedback about the sessions in their entirety. You could leave this task open-ended (e.g., "Write whatever seems important to you about our time together") or you could provide a more focused prompt, or two, such as the following:

- "What will you remember most about our tutoring sessions?"
- "What was your favorite activity during our tutoring sessions this semester? Least favorite?"
- "What did I do this semester that made the most difference in improving your reading and writing?"
- "What suggestions do you have for me for becoming a better tutor in the future?"
- "What advice do you have for me as a future teacher?"

However you focus this task, we suggest scheduling at least a little time—10 or 15 minutes will probably be sufficient—to discuss your tutee's responses with her, because it's possible that she may not elaborate enough in her writing for you to obtain the most useful feedback. In our experience, writing generated in response to these types of prompts serves as an effective springboard for back-and-forth conversation, especially when working with tutees whose poor writing skills may prevent them from saying as eloquently on paper what they might say in person. The value of this writing, however, lies in its permanence (you can refer to it later to reflect on its significance) and its authenticity (the feedback is mostly likely in your tutee's own language and not "translated" by your note-taking procedures).

GETTING FEEDBACK FROM OTHERS AT YOUR SITE

In addition to asking your tutee for evaluative feedback, you might solicit such feedback from others at your tutoring site. Most tutoring programs have such a process built into them, with requirements for tutors to self-evaluate their performance and for supervisors to provide regular response to those self-evaluations and/or their direct observations of tutors at work. For example, mentor teachers and supervisors working with the tutoring program at Grant Middle School in Syracuse, New York, are asked to make comments twice a semester about the following areas of tutors' performances:

- *Punctuality and attendance*: Did the tutor arrive at the tutoring site promptly and consistently? If she missed sessions, did she communicate with people at the site about the absences, and did she make them up responsibly?
- *Preparedness*: Did the tutor come to her sessions with materials ready and formal plans written? Did the plans appear to be appropriate for the student(s)?
- *Rapport*: Did the tutor appear to build a positive relationship with her tutee?
- *Professionalism*: Was the tutor's dress, language, and behavior consistent with the norms of the site? If she is a preservice education student, did she demonstrate a commitment to becoming a teacher during the tutoring?

If your program does not have such a mechanism, you may want to invite your mentor teacher or program director to provide you with some evaluative feedback, either in response to a series of questions like these or perhaps in a more open-ended format such as a letter to you. In some cases, especially if your supervisor is very busy, it may be easier to sit down together and have a conference about your experience, at which time you may want to take notes you can refer to later. Although it can be somewhat nerve-racking to invite others to comment on your performance, we think you'll find this constructive criticism useful, especially if you are planning a career that involves working with young people.

WRITING A CASE STUDY REPORT

If you tutor as part of a university course or clinical experience, it's likely that you will be asked to write a case study report about your tutee. Sometimes volunteers with community-based organizations are asked to do the same, although in these cases the audience for the report is usually the child's family, not an instructor. In the summer clinic that Kathy directs, literacy master's students write case study reports about the children they tutor daily for 6 weeks, and these reports are shared with students' teachers (some of whom referred the students for tutoring in the first place) and with their families. Kathy's students work hard on these documents, revising and editing them many times, because they recognize that the reports make accessible to other people the hard work in which the tutoring pairs engaged over the program.

We expect that you will find writing a case study report to be a terrific way to synthesize and reflect on your entire experience. The process can help you identify specific areas of growth for your student that you might not have recognized before, and it can aid you in thinking through your contributions to this growth. Some tutors we know have been surprised to see how much literacy development took place without their being aware of it, whereas others who were frustrated by their students' seeming lack of progress realized, in the course of writing a report, that their tutees did indeed take some important, albeit small, steps toward becoming more literate.

Just as important, the writing process for a case study report can yield as much insight about tutors as it does about tutees. When Hana Zima, the volunteer whose reflection opens Chapter 4, drafted a report about her tutee, she discovered something new about herself as a reader and learner:

> "My weaknesses as a reader hindered my being able to teach some strategies and other lessons to Gabriel. For example, I think he would benefit from a lesson on highlighting and finding the main points of an article or reading. However, I know now that I am not very good at this—that often I highlight excessively and never find the main point in a book of a chapter, which I don't discover until I go to study for a test or take it."

Having identified and reflected on her own study habits, Hana may be better able to improve *her* learning strategies. Similarly, a graduate student in social studies education, with whom Kelly worked, wrote in his report that he had developed several insights from his tutoring experience that would help him in his future teaching:

> "Though I have only spoken so far in this paper of what I have learned about Jarvis, I have also learned quite a bit about myself as a teacher, especially related to classroom management. During my time with Jarvis, I was tested several times as to how far I would let him go without reining him back in. I found that if I set clear and concise directions at the beginning of the lesson and enforced them, he was less likely to get off topic, and it was easier for me to work with him."

Despite these benefits, some tutors become nervous at the prospect of writing a case study report because they mistakenly believe that they will need to write a document that sounds like a clinical psychologist authored it. We don't see the task this way. Instead, we invite the tutors we work with to write case study reports in a narrative style, using their natural, first-person voices. We want them to include concrete, specific data about students' performances that will be useful to professionals such as teachers, social workers, and program directors, but we don't believe that such professionals will be helped by tutors' adoption of a falsely "objective," distant tone in their writing. Like Peter Johnston (1997), we view case study reports as "simply people describing the activity of people. We cannot avoid interpreting what we observe, so it is proper for us to write reports that sound like an involved person wrote them" (p. 292). Otherwise, tutors run the risk of sending the dangerous and inaccurate message that their judgments about students are *facts*, rather than their particular perspectives in response to the interactions they have had with those young people.

Although the format of your case study report will vary depending upon program expectations, the following advice, adapted from Johnston (1997), should be useful whether you're writing a five- to seven-page paper for a university class, composing a letter to a parent, or completing a standard reporting form adopted by a particular program:

- Avoid using educational jargon that might be confusing or alienating to a family member. If you must use some of this specialized language, be sure to provide clear definitions near the terms. For the most part, though, use the simplest and most direct language possible.
- Don't include anything in your report that you would not be comfortable saying in front of your student. In fact, seriously consider sharing a draft of the report with your tutee to elicit his feedback before you submit the final version.
- Think about how your writing "frames" your tutee. Be especially careful to avoid language that positions your student's struggles with literacy learning as deviations from the ideal or norm, because such stances are rarely helpful in moving a particular student forward.
- Remember as you write that you are creating a document that can have serious consequences for your student. Present your student as a person, not an object, and be sure to focus on his strengths in specific contexts, rather than speaking generally.

Figure 11.1 includes a series of questions that Kelly asks the tutors in her course on literacy across the curriculum to consider while writing their final reports about their students. You may find these questions helpful in conceptualizing what information to include in the various sections of your report, or they may serve as a checklist to help you self-evaluate your written product before you turn it in to an instructor, program director, or, if appropriate, to your student and his family.

BRINGING CLOSURE TO YOUR TUTORING RELATIONSHIP

Writing a case study report is one of the ways you can take stock of your tutoring and reflect on your experience in sum. Remember, too, to build some activities into your last few tutoring sessions—certainly the final one—that will help bring closure to the relationship for your student. If you develop close ties with each other over time, as many tutor–tutee teams do, it may be difficult for both of you to sever them. Anticipate this possibility and plan for it, making it clear to your student that you are not ending your service because of any action on her part but because your course is ending, a cycle of your program is concluding, or you have taken on other responsibilities that prevent you from seeing her on a regular basis. If you can predict the last day of your tutoring experience (e.g., the last day of classes at your university), then we suggest sharing that information at least a few weeks in advance of the date, so that it will not come as a surprise to your student. This is especially important with younger students or those who have experienced a good deal of transience in their lives and may therefore feel abandoned easily.

In addition to talking about closure, you may want to consider creating a memento of your time together. For example, as a final activity in a school-based tutoring program Kathy helped develop, a program assistant took pictures of tutoring pairs at work together and posted them on site, with tutors and tutees each receiving copies. If photos are not taken formally as a part of your program,

As you draft and revise your case study reports, ask yourself the following questions or, better yet, ask someone you trust to read the paper and give you feedback in these areas:

Use of Sources

- Have I backed up my assertions with concrete, specific examples from data collected during my tutoring sessions?
- Do my data come from a wide range of sources (at least three, if not more), and are those sources clearly labeled in the paper?

Content

- Does my paper demonstrate how well I've come to know my tutee as a literacy learner?
- Have I balanced my attention to my tutee's strengths, needs, and areas of growth?
- Have I laid out recommendations for others' future work with my tutee that build on his or her strengths and begin to address some of his or her needs as a literacy learner?

Awareness of Audience

- Would my tutee's classroom teacher or parent be able to recognize him or her from my descriptions?
- Have I written the paper in a respectful enough way that I would feel comfortable if my tutee read it?
- Have I eliminated or defined educational jargon clearly enough in the paper that it won't be off-putting to people who are not educators?

Quality of Writing

- Is my paper written clearly? Will my main points be clear to the reader?
- Does my paper have a logical structure? Does it flow well from section to section?
- Is my paper conventionally edited? Have I eliminated any errors that might distract the reader from my message?

FIGURE 11.1. Questions to guide case study reports.

you could bring a camera to your last session (even a disposable one would do the trick) and ask someone to snap a picture of you and your tutee for each of you. Be mindful if you do so, however, of rules in your context governing the public use of such photographs; whether it would be appropriate to include one or more of them in a document such as a course portfolio will depend on the expectations at your site.

In addition to, or in lieu of, a photograph, a small gift might be appropriate. (Again, check with your mentor teacher or program director to find out what the norms are in this area.) As a way to encourage reading for pleasure beyond your formal tutoring, you might purchase a paperback book or a magazine subscription for your student that reflects her interests, and you might want to inscribe the book with a personal message. Less expensive but just as meaningful is a card or letter to your tutee expressing final sentiments and, if you wish, providing your student with a postal or e-mail address, should she want to keep in touch with you. Whatever you decide to do, do not underestimate the significance that even these small gestures can have in marking the end of your time with your tutee, even if she may not show her appreciation in dramatic ways.

REFLECTING BEYOND THE TUTORING EXPERIENCE

Finally, we invite you to think about your tutoring experience in ways that transcend a relationship with a particular student. Many of those who serve as literacy tutors to adolescents are enrolled in university programs meant to certify them as teachers in secondary content areas such as math, social studies, or English. If you fit this profile, we urge you to reflect on your tutoring experience in light of your future teaching. Part of the reason that many education programs, including the ones in which we teach, place such a high premium on field placements is that they allow future teachers to integrate knowledge and skills from their on-campus course work with insights from work with students—real ones, who have real dreams and histories and idiosyncrasies.

As you consider the professional implications of your tutoring in light of other learning opportunities in your program, you might ask yourself one or more of the following questions:

- "What have I learned about adolescents' developmental needs, interests, and attitudes from my tutoring experience that will inform my future interactions and relationships with students?"
- "What have I learned from this experience that will help me promote my students' literacy development in whatever content area I teach?"
- "Whose expertise can I draw on, in and out of school, to help support struggling literacy learners? With whom can I collaborate in this important endeavor?"
- "What will I need to do, when teaching classes of 20–30 students, to enact the principles and practices—or modified versions of them—that I've found to be effective with my individual tutee or pair of tutees?"
- "In what ways might middle and high schools need to change in order to serve the needs of students such as my tutee better in the future? How can I be a part of that change?"

If you are a volunteer tutor not enrolled in an education program, you, too, will want to reflect on the implications of your experience, but the questions you ask yourself will undoubtedly be different. The two of us began to think more explicitly about these issues this past fall, when we attended a luncheon at Syracuse University where the featured speaker was Wendy Kopp, the founder of Teach for America, a service corps dedicated to placing college graduates with various majors in underserved rural and urban schools. Acknowledging that not all alumni of the program would remain in the classroom beyond their 2-year commitment, Kopp argued that those who eventually left teaching had an important role to play as advocates for public education in whatever field they entered next. She echoed the language of the Teach for America website (*www.teachforamerica.org*), which contends that members' intense experiences as part of the corps can help them learn to be "lifelong leaders in the effort to expand opportunity for children."

Without coming down on one side or the other of debates surrounding Teach for America's effectiveness as a teacher preparation program, we want to suggest here that a similar perspective may be useful for volunteers who tutor adolescent literacy learners. Even if you never become a teacher, we hope that the insights you glean from your experience will make you more sensitive to the challenges faced by adolescents, their families, their teachers, and other advocates in creating vibrant learning communities that enable all young people to grow and flourish. We hope that greater awareness of these issues will make you interested in learning more about public education and/or community-based service organizations as well as more likely to support such endeavors in the future with your time, money, and energy.

More specifically, we hope that your tutoring will convince you of the importance of supporting initiatives aligned with the principles outlined in the International Reading Association's (IRA) position statement on adolescent literacy (Moore et al., 1999), the document we quoted at the beginning of this book. As the authors of this statement noted, far more public attention has been paid to reading acquisition and instruction for students in grades K–3 than for older learners. Only when we develop what the IRA commission calls a "comprehensive effort" (p. 4) to provide all students with access to materials, quality instruction, and support will we truly have the kinds of literacy-rich classrooms, schools, and communities that adolescent learners so obviously deserve. We congratulate you for taking steps to provide these conditions by becoming a literacy tutor, and we send you our best wishes for your success in that important endeavor.

APPENDICES

APPENDIX A

Recommended Resources

Resources on Struggling Adolescent Literacy Learners

Allen, J. (2000). *Yellow brick roads: Shared and guided paths to independent reading, 4–12.* Portland, ME: Stenhouse.

Alvermann, D., Moore, D., & Hinchman, K. (2000). *Struggling adolescent readers: A collection of teaching strategies.* Newark, DE: International Reading Association.

Ash, G. E. (2002, March). Teaching readers who struggle: A pragmatic middle school framework. *Reading Online, 5*(7). Available online at *http://www.readingonline.org/articles/art_index.asp?HREF=ash/index.html*

Beers, K. (2003). *When kids can't read, what teachers can do: A guide for teachers, 6–12.* Portsmouth, NH: Heinemann.

Fisher, D., & Frey, N. (2003). Writing instruction for struggling adolescent readers. *Journal of Adolescent and Adult Literacy, 46*(5), 396–405.

Harvey, S., & Goudvis, A. (2000). *Strategies that work: Teaching comprehension to enhance understanding.* Portland, ME: Stenhouse.

Ivey, G. (1999). Reflections on teaching struggling middle school readers. *Journal of Adolescent and Adult Literacy, 42*(5), 372–381.

Moore, D., Bean, T., Birdyshaw, D., & Rycik, J. (1999). *Adolescent literacy: A position statement.* Newark, DE: International Reading Association. Available online at *http://www.reading.org/positions/adol_lit.html*

Moore, D., & Hinchman, K. (2002). *Starting out: A guide to teaching adolescents who struggle with reading.* Boston: Allyn & Bacon.

Schoenbach, R., Greenleaf, C., Cziko, C., & Hurwitz, L. (1999). *Reading for understanding: A guide for improving reading in middle and high school classrooms.* San Francisco: Jossey-Bass.

Tovani, C. (2000). *I read it but I don't get it: Comprehension strategies for adolescent readers.* Portland, ME: Stenhouse.

Worthy, J., Broaddus, K., & Ivey, G. (2001). *Pathways to independence: Reading, writing, and learning in grades 3–8.* New York: Guilford Press.

Resources on Literacy Tutoring

Cheatham, J. B. (1998). *Help a child learn to read*. Washington, DC: Literacy Volunteers of America. (See also the Literacy Volunteers of America website at *http://www.literacyvolunteers.org/ppe/index.html*)

Cobb, J., & Allen, D. (2001). When a criminal justice major becomes an America Reads tutor: A case study. *Journal of Adolescent and Adult Literacy, 44*(6), 556–564.

Johnston, F. R., Invernizzi, M., & Juel, C. (1998*). Book buddies: Guidelines for volunteer tutors of emergent and early readers*. New York: Guilford Press.

Morris, D. (1999). *The Howard Street tutoring manual: Teaching at-risk readers in the primary grades*. New York: Guilford Press.

Morrow, L. M., & Woo, D. G. (2000). *Tutoring programs for struggling readers: The America Reads challenge*. New York: Guilford Press.

Roller, C. (1998). *So . . . what's a tutor to do?* Newark, DE: International Reading Association.

Schumm, J. S., & Schumm, G., Jr. (1999). *The reading tutor's handbook: A commonsense guide to helping students read and write*. Minneapolis, MN: Free Spirit.

Wasik, B. (1998). Using volunteers as reading tutors: Guidelines for successful practices. *The Reading Teacher, 51,* 562–570.

Blank Session Planning and Reflection Form

Tutor: _____ Tutee(s): _____

Date: _____ Session #: _____

1. Literacy Focus for Lesson (check no more than one or two)

___ Making connections   ___ Developing fluency

___ Asking questions   ___ Considering a model for writing task

___ Visualizing   ___ Planning/prewriting

___ Predicting/inferring   ___ Organizing writing

___ Determining important ___ Adding supporting details
    ideas/summarizing

___ Dealing with vocabulary ___ Editing for grammar/spelling

2. Session Goals/Objectives (no more than two or three)

3. Texts/Materials

(continued)

4. Procedures for Session Activities

5. Plans for Assessing Progress toward Session Goals/Objectives

6. Postsession Reflection

Sample Planning and Reflection Forms Completed by Tutors

Example 1

Tutor: <u>Melissa Porter</u>　　　Tutee(s): <u>Seth</u>

Date: <u>10/8</u>　　　Session #: <u>2</u>

1. Literacy Focus for Lesson (check no more than one or two)

_X_ Making connections	___ Developing fluency
___ Asking questions	___ Considering a model for writing task
___ Visualizing	___ Planning/prewriting
___ Predicting/inferring	___ Organizing writing
___ Determining important ideas/summarizing	___ Adding supporting details
___ Dealing with vocabulary	___ Editing for grammar/spelling

2. Session Goals/Objectives (no more than two or three)

- To introduce, and hopefully pique interest in, both the poetry of a classic author and a recent poet/rapper.
- To work on the skill of comparing/contrasting by closely reading poems by two authors and identifying the differences and similarities.

3. Texts/Materials

- Paper
- Pencil
- *The Panther and the Lash: Poems of Our Times,* by Langston Hughes
- *The Rose That Grew from Concrete,* by Tupac Shakur

(continued)

4. Procedures for Session Activities

- Show the text choices and explain why I chose them.
- Check for prior knowledge about Langston Hughes and provide a little more if he needs it.
- Read "Dream Deferred" aloud to him and talk a little bit about what we think it means.
- Discuss Seth's prior knowledge about Tupac Shakur, then read "A Love Unspoken" together.
- Talk about similarities between the two poets and poems.
- Talk about differences between the two poets and poems.
- Invite Seth to choose poems from each collection that interest him and read them aloud to me, then discuss them in whatever time is left.

5. Plans for Assessing Progress toward Session Goals/Objectives

- Take notes about how Seth compares and contrasts the two poems and the poets.
- Record which poems he chooses on his own.

6. Postsession Reflection

Tutoring went OK today. Seth is sort of a ho-hum kind of guy—nothing seems that big a deal to him. He was reluctant about Langston Hughes, I think because he didn't know much about him and wasn't familiar with his background. When I told him Hughes was an African American poet, one of the most well known, he seemed a little more interested. "Dream Deferred" held his attention for a short time, but he didn't want to discuss it for long. When I pulled out the book of poetry by Tupac, his eyes lit up and he smiled, I think, because he realized I had been paying attention to what he was interested in. He was pretty happy to browse quietly, and I asked him to choose a favorite and read it out loud. He remained interested in reading to himself, and when I asked him if he wanted to read aloud more, he said no. After a while, though, we found a short poem he read aloud, and I told him the poem sounded better to me when I heard him read it. He began to read several to me, and very well. We talked a bit about why Tupac wrote poetry and how his poetry was different from rap music but similar, and how Hughes could be compared to Tupac. Seth makes great connections and has great ideas about poetry. He wants to know how Langston Hughes died. I asked him if he might be interested in talking about and reading rap lyrics next visit—he was pretty excited about that.

Example 2

Tutor: _Nathan Coolidge_   Tutee(s): _Erica & Randy_

Date: _10/22_   Session #: _5_

1. Literacy Focus for Lesson (check no more than one or two)

   ___ Making connections   ___ Developing fluency

   _X_ Asking questions   ___ Considering a model for writing task

   ___ Visualizing   ___ Planning/prewriting

   _X_ Predicting/inferring   ___ Organizing writing

   ___ Determining important   ___ Adding supporting details
         ideas/summarizing

   ___ Dealing with vocabulary   ___ Editing for grammar/spelling

2. Session Goals/Objectives (no more than two or three)

- Continue to work on the strategy of prediction.
- Get students to focus on asking themselves prediction questions instead of plowing through the text simply using decoding skills.

3. Texts/Materials

- Photocopies of "Caught in the Act" by Tom and Pat Leeson from *Natural Wildlife*. The first photocopy will be cut into sections, and the remaining two will be for tutees to take home with them.
- The activity also requires a pencil and a piece of paper.

4. Procedures for Session Activities

- Review the strategy of prediction with Erica and Randy.
- Introduce the article with a brief description of where I found it, and why I felt we should investigate it.
- Show them the title of the article and have them make predictions about the story from the information in the title.
- Have Erica or Randy read aloud the first snippet of text. After the reading is complete, they can revisit their predictions to find out if they were correct. We will make predictions about the rest of the text. Some questions to keep in mind: Who are the narrators? What is their profession? How does the title of the article relate to their profession?
- Have the person who did not read section 1 read section 2. Repeat the procedure. Make sure to ask them to describe their rationales for the predictions they make.
- Follow up with a debriefing on how well their predictions fit with the facts of the text. Discuss what specific factors led to their need to revise their predictions. Ask how this activity could help them in Ms. Heron's class.
- Finish the session with silent reading from a book of their choice.

(continued)

5. Plans for Assessing Progress toward Session Goals/Objectives

- Observe and record students' predictions and questions about the text.
- See if a noticeable improvement has been made in the strategy of prediction since the last session. Are they slowing down to examine the information in the text? Are they making any connections to the text?

6. Postsession Reflection

After the last session, I felt that both Erica and Randy did not fully understand the concept of prediction or its usefulness as a comprehension strategy. They wanted to read the story to get it over with as quickly as possible, instead of reading the story to gain new information. Today I wanted to slow down their reading, so I took the text and cut it into chunks (as Allen recommends in *Yellow Brick Roads*) that could be easily discussed without the distraction of the rest of the text.

This exercise seemed to be more successful for Erica and Randy. Erica asked a few questions, made more predictions, and was generally more engaged than Randy, though. He felt the need to constantly stand up or move around, causing the activity to come to a halt as I tried to get him to stay focused on the task. I'm not sure whether it is the texts I choose or just that Randy is reluctant to do work related to school.

During the silent reading at the end of the session, Randy could not wait to show me a multipage ad about a Japanese animation cartoon he watches on TV. The ad showed a picture of all the characters, with a brief bio of each underneath. I asked him to read some of the bios to me. He managed to do so with an above-average level of fluency, even though the text contained some fairly challenging vocabulary, such as *telekinetic* and *philosopher*. He also had more Yuh-Gi-Oh cards with him today. I asked him to explain them to me. Give me a break: Those things are so complicated, I have no idea how he remembers all those rules. There must be a way to incorporate his knowledge of those cards into a demonstration about literacy skills.

Example 3

Tutor: _Andrew Brechko_   Tutee(s): _Jimmy_

Date: _11/20_   Session #: _7_

1. Literacy Focus for Lesson (check no more than one or two)

___ Making connections	___ Developing fluency
___ Asking questions	___ Considering a model for writing task
___ Visualizing	___ Planning/prewriting
___ Predicting/inferring	_X_ Organizing writing
_X_ Determining important ideas/summarizing	___ Adding supporting details
___ Dealing with vocabulary	___ Editing for grammar/spelling

2. Session Goals/Objectives (no more than two or three)
- To conduct some Internet research on a rifle from World War II.
- Work on summarizing by reading information from the Web, summarizing it aloud, and then writing a paragraph describing the rifle.

3. Texts/Materials
- Computer
- Website (I researched the rifle ahead of time and wrote down the URL for the website)
- Pen and paper

4. Procedures for Session Activities
- Go online together and find the website with the history of the German rifle Jimmy's uncle has from World War II.
- Find information about the rifle on the site and read it together, summarizing the main points as we go, with Jimmy taking the lead on this as we move through the text.
- Have Jimmy write a paragraph about how his uncle got the rifle in the first place, and then describe the history of the weapon and its nomenclature.

5. Plans for Assessing Progress toward Session Goals/Objectives
- Observe how Jimmy reads the text when it is his turn and how he explains the main points; pay attention to when he needs help.
- Look at the quality of the summary writing he does about the rifle, based on his notes.

(continued)

6. Postsession Reflection

Today Jimmy read about a family heirloom (Mauser 98K 8mm rifle) he had told me about in an earlier session. He was very excited because this project had to do with his family's history. He did very well when reading the text and summarizing/picking out the main points. I was very impressed with his ability. He needed very little help from me and only checked with me when he wanted to confirm his ideas. He was really excited to go home and share his findings about the rifle with his grandfather. When it came to actually writing the paragraph, he needed some motivation. I find that to be the hardest thing about working with Jimmy: He doesn't like to write. He whines and procrastinates when I ask him to do certain writing tasks. I feel like he has done really well with his war portfolio (I think that he has a sense of accomplishment and feels good about what we have done), but I wish he would realize how important it is for written expression to complement the drawing he's so good at.

APPENDIX D

Tips for Mentor Teachers
Who Work with Tutors

Suggestions for Selecting Tutees and Supporting Tutors

If you are responsible for selecting the student or students with whom tutors will work, you will want to consider the following:

1. *Choose a student whose attendance is regular enough to be benefited by one-on-one help.* In many cases, students' attendance improves on tutoring days because they do not want to miss the extra attention. You may find that selecting an occasionally absent student for tutoring will help with this problem. That said, tutors won't learn much about literacy or be able to provide much assistance if the students they're assigned do not come to school on a regular basis. Try to strike a balance on this issue when recommending students to be tutored.

2. *Choose a child whose behavior is manageable by a new teacher.* Tutors don't expect "perfect" behavior, and the one-on-one setting should make management easier, but please keep in mind that tutors, even those enrolled in preservice education programs, often have limited experience dealing with challenging behavior.

3. *Choose a child who needs help with comprehension and fluency, rather than basic decoding.* As volunteers or future content-area teachers (not reading specialists), the tutees are learning about ways to support literacy development, not usually about remediation per se. They will likely know a fair amount about comprehension and composing strategies from their training and the reading of this book, but they will know far less about phonics or decoding.

4. *Keep the focus on literacy development.* Although tutors expect to help with homework and give moral support on occasion, the focus of the sessions should be on reading and writing practice and strategy development. It is our hope that students' confidence, interest in literacy, fluency, and comprehension will improve through the one-on-one interactions, not just that they will complete more assignments or talk with tutors about personal problems.

5. *Provide tutors with age-appropriate materials related to your curriculum or content area.* Although tutors will likely have access to various texts through their participation

161

in their tutoring program, they will benefit from your suggestions of texts that their tutee might learn from or enjoy. When you are going to begin a particular area of study, for example, tutoring pairs could read some material on that subject to build background knowledge for the tutee.

6. *Communicate with tutors about any skills or strategies you'd like them to focus on in their sessions.* If you see that the tutee struggles with metacognition or prior knowledge activation, you can suggest that as a focus for a session, or series of sessions, with the tutee.

7. *Adjust expectations for tutees if they leave the classroom for tutoring.* Struggling literacy learners, especially those who are at risk academically, often resent, or balk at, attending their literacy tutoring sessions, despite their need for them, if they feel that missing class puts them further behind in a particular subject. Consider reducing the volume of classwork you expect from them on their tutoring days, or negotiate how tutors can integrate some of that material into their sessions. Do not simply double their homework by assigning them to do missed class assignments independently, because such an action is likely to undermine their motivation to participate in tutoring.

Ways to Involve Literacy Tutors in Your Classes

In addition to their regular literacy tutoring, you might invite tutors to do any of the following during their time with you, depending on your needs and their comfort level:

- Take attendance and/or return assignments so that they can learn students' names.
- Do a read-aloud of a short text (e.g., a newspaper article, a short story, a picture book) at the beginning of a class.
- Take notes about participation during a whole-class activity you're leading.
- Take focused notes on the participation or performance of a particular student (e.g., one you're concerned about, one you want to get to know better, their tutee) or group of students.
- Circulate the room and provide assistance as students work independently.
- Sit at a designated help desk where individual students can come to receive assistance on an assignment.
- Monitor and participate in a particular group during a cooperative activity or literature circle.
- Lead a group discussion or a guided reading of a particular text (with the latter, they will need some direction).
- Confer with individual students on a piece of writing or a project in progress.
- Read to, or with, individual students who struggle, including (but not limited to) their own tutees.
- Accompany individual students or groups of students to the library or computer lab to do research.
- Assist students working on research projects or writing assignments in one of your teammates' classrooms.
- Gather materials (e.g., picture books, websites, newspaper articles) for a lesson or unit you're planning to teach.
- Prepare, with your help, a short lesson and teach it. (This might be more appropriate toward the end of their time with you, when they are more experienced and confident.)

References

Allen, J. (1999). *Words, words, words: Teaching vocabulary in grades 4–12*. Portland, ME: Stenhouse.

Allen, J. (2000). *Yellow brick roads: Shared and guided paths to independent literacy, 4–12*. Portland, ME: Stenhouse.

Allen, J. (2004). *Tools for teaching content literacy*. York, ME: Stenhouse.

Allen, J., & Gonzalez, K. (1998). *There's room for me here: Literacy workshop in the middle school*. York, ME: Stenhouse.

Allen, J., Michalove, B., & Shockley, B. (1993). *Engaging children: Community and chaos in the lives of young literacy learners*. Portsmouth, NH: Heinemann.

Allington, R. L. (1983). Fluency: The neglected goal. *The Reading Teacher, 36*, 556–561.

Allington, R. L. (2001). *What really matters for struggling readers: Designing research-based programs*. New York: Longman.

Alvermann, D. E. (2001). Reading adolescents' reading identities: Looking back to look ahead. *Journal of Adolescent and Adult Literacy, 44*, 676–690.

Alvermann, D. E. (2002). *Adolescents and literacies in a digital world*. New York: Peter Lang.

Alvermann, D. E., & Phelps, S. (2002). *Content reading and literacy: Succeeding in today's diverse classrooms* (3rd ed.). Boston: Allyn & Bacon.

Anderson, R., Wilson, P., & Fielding, L. (1988). Growth in reading and how children spend their time outside of school. *Reading Research Quarterly, 23*, 285–303.

Atwell, N. (1998). *In the middle: New understandings about writing, reading, and learning* (2nd ed.). Portsmouth, NH: Heinemann.

Barry, A. L. (2002). Reading strategies teachers say they use. *Journal of Adolescent and Adult Literacy, 46*, 132–141.

Baumann, J., Jones, L., & Seifert-Kessell, N. (1999). Using think alouds to enhance children's comprehension monitoring abilities. In R. Allington (Ed.), *Teaching struggling readers: Advice from* The Reading Teacher (pp. 187–199). Newark, DE: International Reading Association.

Beers, K. (2003). *When kids can't read, what teachers can do: A guide for teachers, 6–12*. Portsmouth, NH: Heinemann.

Betts, E. A. (1957). *Foundations of reading instruction.* New York: American Book Company. (Original work published 1946)

Bigelow, B., Christensen, L., Karp, S., Miner, B., & Peterson, B. (1994). *Rethinking our classrooms: Teaching for equity and justice.* Milwaukee, WI: Rethinking Schools.

Bintz, W. P. (1993). Resistant readers in secondary education: Some insights and implications. *Journal of Reading, 36,* 604–615.

Blachman, B., Tangel, D., Ball, E. W., Black, R., & McGraw, C. K. (1999). Developing phonological awareness and word recognition skills: A two-year intervention with low-income, inner-city children. *Reading and Writing: An Interdisciplinary Journal, 11,* 239–273.

Blachowicz, C. L. Z., & Fisher, P. J. L. (1996). *Teaching vocabulary in all classrooms.* Columbus, OH: Merrill.

Bomer, R. (1999). Conferring with struggling readers: The test of our craft, courage, and hope. *The New Advocate, 12,* 21–38.

Calkins, L. (1986). *The art of teaching writing.* Portsmouth, NH: Heinemann.

Chandler, K. (2000). What I wish I'd known about teaching spelling. *English Journal, 89,* 87–95.

Chandler, K., and The Mapleton Teacher-Research Group. (1999). *Spelling inquiry: How one elementary school caught the mnemonic plague.* York, ME: Stenhouse.

Chandler-Olcott, K., & Mahar, D. (2003). Adolescents' anime-inspired fanfictions: An exploration of multiliteracies. *Journal of Adolescent and Adult Literacy, 46*(7), 556–566.

Cheatham, J. B. (1998). *Help a child learn to read.* Washington, DC: George Washington University, Region III Comprehensive Center, and Literacy Volunteers of America.

Cheatham, J. B., Colvin, R. J., & Laminack, L. (1993). *Tutor: A collaborative approach to literacy instruction* (7th ed.). Syracuse, NY: Literacy Volunteers of America.

Christenbury, L. (2000). *Making the journey: Being and becoming a teacher of English language arts* (2nd ed.). Portsmouth, NH: Heinemann.

Clay, M. M. (1993). *Reading recovery: A guidebook for teachers in training.* Portsmouth, NH: Heinemann.

Cole, A. D. (2002). *Better answers: Written performance that looks good and sounds smart.* Portland, ME: Stenhouse.

Daniels, H., Bizar, M., & Zemelman, S. (2001). *Rethinking high school: Best practice in teaching, learning, and leadership.* Portsmouth, NH: Heinemann.

Delpit, L. (2003). Educators as "seed people" growing a new future. *Educational Researcher, 32,* 14–21.

Dole, J., Duffy, G., Roehler, L., & Pearson, P. D. (1991). Moving from the old to the new: Research on reading comprehension instruction. *Review of Educational Research, 61,* 239–264.

Donald, D. H. (1996). *Why the north won the Civil War.* New York: Simon & Schuster.

Duke, C., & Sanchez, R. (2000). *Assessing writing across the curriculum.* Chapel Hill, NC: Carolina Academic Press.

Emig, J. (1971). *The composing processes of twelfth graders.* Urbana, IL: National Council of Teachers of English.

Finders, M. (1997). *Just girls: Hidden literacies and life in junior high.* New York: Teachers College Press.

Fisher, D. (2001). "We're moving on up": Creating a school wide literacy effort in an urban high school. *Journal of Adolescent and Adult Literacy, 45,* 92–101.

Fisher, D., Frey, N., & Williams. D. (2002). Seven literacy strategies that work. *Educational Leadership, 60,* 70–73.

Fletcher, R., & Portalupi, J. (1998). *Craft lessons: Teaching writing K–8.* York, ME: Stenhouse.

Flower, L., & Hayes, J. (1977). Problem-solving strategies and the writing process. *College English, 39,* 449–461.

Fountas, I., & Pinnell, G. S. (2001). *Creating readers and writers, Grades 3–6.* Portsmouth, NH: Heinemann.

Fry, E., Kress, J., & Fountoukidis, D. (1993). *The reading teacher's book of lists* (3rd ed.). Englewood Cliffs, NJ: Prentice-Hall.

Fullan, M. (2001). *Leading in a culture of change.* San Francisco: Jossey-Bass.

Gambrell, L., & Jawitz, P. (1999). Mental imagery, text illustrations, and children's story comprehension and recall. *Reading Research Quarterly, 28,* 264–276.

Gaskins, R. W., Gaskins, J. C., & Gaskins, I. W. (1991). A decoding program for poor readers–and the rest of the class too! *Language Arts, 68,* 213–225.

Gavelek, J., Raphael, T., Biondo, S., & Wang, D. (2000). Integrated literacy instruction. In M. Kamil, P. Mosenthal, P. D. Pearson, & R. Barr (Eds.), *Handbook of reading research* (Vol. 3, pp. 587–607). Mahwah, NJ: Erlbaum.

Gee, J. P. (2001). Reading as situated language: A sociocognitive perspective. *Journal of Adolescent and Adult Literacy, 44,* 714–725.

Gee, J. P. (2003). *What video games have to teach us about literacy and learning.* New York: Palgrave MacMillan.

Gere, A. R. (1985). *Roots in the sawdust: Writing to learn across the disciplines.* Urbana, IL: National Council of Teachers of English.

Goodlad, J. I. (1984). *A place called school: Promise for the future.* New York: McGraw-Hill.

Goodman, Y., Watson, D., & Burke, C. (1987). *Reading miscue inventory: Alternative procedures.* New York: Richard C. Owens.

Gordon, K. E. (1993). *The new well-tempered sentence: A punctuation handbook for the innocent, the eager, and the doomed.* New York: Ticknor & Fields.

Graves, D. (1983). *Writing: Teachers and children at work.* Portsmouth, NH: Heinemann.

Hale, C. (1999). *Sin and syntax: How to craft wickedly effective prose.* New York: Broadway.

Harvey, S., & Goudvis, A. (2000). *Strategies that work: Teaching comprehension to enhance understanding.* York, ME: Stenhouse.

Hinchman, K. A., Alvermann, D. E., Boyd, F., Brozo, W., & Vacca, R. (2003). Supporting older students' in- and out-of-school literacies. *Journal of Adolescent and Adult Literacy, 47,* 304–310.

Hinchman, K. A., & Zalewski, P. (1996). Reading for success in a tenth-grade global studies class: A qualitative study. *Journal of Literacy Research, 26,* 91–106.

Hopkins, G., & Bean, T. (1999). Vocabulary learning with the verbal–visual word association strategy in a Native American community. *Journal of Adolescent and Adult Literacy, 42*(4), 272–281.

Hubbard, R. S. (1993). Seeing what is not seen: Another reason for writing up teacher research. *Teacher Research: The Journal of Classroom Inquiry, 1*(1), 143–147.

Hughes, M., & Searle, D. (1997). *The violent E and other tricky sounds: Learning to spell from kindergarten through grade 6.* York, ME: Stenhouse.

Hyerle, D. (1996). *Visual tools for constructing knowledge.* Alexandria, VA: Association for Supervision and Curriculum Development.

Ivey, G., & Broaddus, K. (2001). "Just plain reading": A survey of what makes students want to read in middle school classrooms. *Reading Research Quarterly, 36,* 350–377.

Johnson, M., Kress, R., & Pikulski, J. (1987). *Informal reading inventories* (2nd ed.). Newark: DE: International Reading Association.

Johnston, P. (1997). *Knowing literacy: Constructive literacy assessment.* York, ME: Stenhouse.

Jorgensen, C. (1998). *Restructuring high schools for all students: Taking inclusion to the next level.* Baltimore: Paul Brookes.

Keene, E., & Zimmermann, S. (1997). *Mosaic of thought: Teaching comprehension in a reader's workshop*. Portsmouth, NH: Heinemann.

Knobel, M., & Lankshear, C. (2002). Cut, paste, publish: The production and consumption of 'zines. In D. E. Alvermann (Ed.), *Adolescents and literacies in a digital world* (pp. 164–185) New York: Peter Lang.

Koskinen, P., Gambrell, L., Kapinus, B., & Heathington, B. (1988). Retelling: A strategy for enhancing students' reading comprehension. *The Reading Teacher, 41*(5), 892–897.

Krashen, S. (1993). *The power of reading: Insights from the research*. Englewood, CO: Libraries Unlimited.

Langer, J. (2001). Succeeding against the odds in English. *English Journal, 91*(1), 37–42.

Lederer, R., & Dowis, R. (2001). *Sleeping dogs don't lay: Practical advice for the grammatically challenged*. New York: St. Martin's Press.

Lesko, N. (2000). *Act your age: A cultural construction of adolescence*. New York: Routledge Falmer.

Lewis, C., & Fabos, B. (1999, December). *Chatting on-line: Uses of instant message communication among adolescent girls*. Paper presented at the annual meeting of the National Reading Conference, Orlando, FL.

Lipson, M., & Wixson, K. (1996). *Assessment and instruction of reading and writing difficulty: An interactive approach* (2nd ed.). New York: Allyn & Bacon.

Luke, A., (2000). Critical literacy in Australia: A matter of context and standpoint. *Journal of Adolescent and Adult Literacy, 43*, 448–461.

McFedries, P. (2004). *Word spy: The word lover's guide to modern culture*. New York: Broadway.

McKeown, M. G., Beck, I. L., & Sinatra, G. M. (1992). The contribution of prior knowledge and coherent text to comprehension. *Reading Research Quarterly, 27*, 79–93.

Meyer, M. S., & Felton, R. H. (1999). Repeated reading to enhance fluency: Old approaches and new directions. *Annals of Dyslexia, 49*, 283–306.

Michel, P. (1994). *The child's view of reading: Understandings for teachers and parents*. Boston: Allyn & Bacon.

Miller, D. (2002). *Reading with meaning: Teaching comprehension in the primary grades*. Portland, ME: Stenhouse.

Moats, L. (2001). When older students can't read. *Educational Leadership, 58*, 36–40.

Moje, E. B. (2000a). *All the stories we have: Adolescents' insights about literacy and learning in secondary schools*. Newark, DE: International Reading Association.

Moje, E. B. (2000b). "To be part of the story": The literacy practices of gangsta adolescents. *Teachers College Record, 102*, 651–690.

Moline, S. (1995). *I see what you mean: Children at work with visual information*. York, ME: Stenhouse.

Moore, D., Bean, T., Birdyshaw, D., & Rycik, J. (1999). *Adolescent literacy: A position statement*. Newark, DE: International Reading Association.

Moore, D., & Hinchman, K. A. (2002). *Starting out: A guide to teaching adolescents who struggle with reading*. New York: Allyn & Bacon.

Mora, J. (2001–2002). Responding to the demographic challenge: An Internet classroom for teachers of language-minority students. *Reading Online, 4*(5). Retrieved online from *http://www.readingonline.org/electronic/elec_index.asp?HREF=/electronic/mora/index.html*

Morris, D. (1999). *The Howard Street tutoring manual: Teaching at-risk readers in the primary grades*. New York: Guilford Press.

Morrow, L. M. (1986). Effects of structural guidance in story retelling on children's dictation. *Journal of Reading Behavior, 18*, 135–152.

Murray, D. (1985). *A writer teaches writing.* Boston: Houghton Mifflin.

National Center for Educational Statistics. (2003). *The nation's report card.* Washington, DC: Author. Retrieved at *http://nces.ed.gov/nationsreportcard*

National Reading Panel. (2000). *Teaching children to read: An evidence-based assessment of the scientific research literature on reading and its implications for reading instruction.* Washington, DC: National Institute of Child Health and Human Development (National Institutes of Health, U.S. Department of Health and Human Services).

Nilsen, A. P., & Nilsen, D. F. (2002). Lessons in the teaching of vocabulary from September 11 and Harry Potter. *Journal of Adolescent and Adult Literacy, 46*(3), 254–260.

Ogle, D. (1986). K-W-L: A teaching model that develops active reading in expository text. *The Reading Teacher, 39*(6), 564–570.

Palinscar, A. M., & Brown, A. (1984). Reciprocal teaching of comprehension-fostering and comprehension-monitoring activities. *Cognition and Instruction, 1,* 117–175.

Pearson, P. D., & Fielding, L. (1991). Comprehension instruction. In R. Barr, M. Kamil, P. Mosenthal, & P. D. Pearson (Eds.), *Handbook of reading research* (Vol. 2, pp. 815–860). New York: Longman.

Pearson, P. D., & Fielding, L. (1994). Reading comprehension: What works—synthesis of research. *Educational Leadership, 51,* 62–68.

Pearson, P. D., & Gallagher, M. C. (1983). The instruction of reading comprehension. *Contemporary Educational Psychology, 8,* 317–344.

Pressley, M. (2002). *Reading instruction that works: The case for balanced teaching* (2nd ed.). New York: Guilford Press.

Raphael, T. (1984). Teaching learners about sources of information for answering comprehension questions. *Journal of Reading, 27,* 303–311.

Rhodes, L. K., & Nathenson-Mejia, S. (1992). Anecdotal records: A powerful tool for ongoing literacy assessment. *The Reading Teacher, 45,* 502–509.

Rief, L. (1992). *Seeking diversity: Language arts with adolescents.* Portsmouth, NH: Heinemann.

Riggs, E. G., & Serafin, A. G. (1998). The principal as instructional leader: Teaching high school teachers how to teach reading. *NASSP Bulletin, 82*(600), 78–84.

Roller, C. (1998). *So, what's a tutor to do?* Newark, DE: International Reading Association.

Ruddell, M. R., & Shearer, B. A. (2002). "Extraordinary," "tremendous," "exhilarating," "magnificent": Middle school at-risk students become avid word learners with the Vocabulary Self-Collection Strategy. *Journal of Adolescent and Adult Literacy, 45,* 352–366.

Rycik, J. (1998). From information to interaction: Involving parents in the literacy development of their adolescent. *NASSP Bulletin, 82*(600), 67–72.

Ryder, R. J., & Graves, M. (1998). *Reading and learning in content areas* (2nd ed.). Upper Saddle River, NJ: Merrill.

Samuels, S. J. (1979). The method of repeated readings. *The Reading Teacher, 32,* 403–408.

Santa, C. M., Havens, L. T., & Maycumber, E. M (1996). *Project CRISS: Creating independence through student owned strategies.* Dubuque, IA: Kendall/Hunt.

Schoenbach, R., Greenleaf, C., Cziko, C., & Hurwitz, L. (1999). *Reading for understanding: A guide to improving reading in middle and high school classrooms.* San Francisco: Jossey-Bass.

Schultz, K. (2002). Looking across space and time: Reconceptualizing literacy learning in and out of school. *Research in the Teaching of English, 36,* 356–390.

Shaughnessy, M. (1977). *Errors and expectations: A guide for the teacher of basic writing.* New York: Oxford University Press.

Shaywitz, S. (2003). *Overcoming dyslexia: A new and complete science-based program for overcoming reading problems at any level.* New York: Alfred Knopf.

Singer, H., & Donlan, D. (1982). Active comprehension: Problem-solving schema with question generation for comprehension of complex short stories. *Reading Research Quarterly, 17,* 166–185.

Singer, H., & Donlan, D. (1989). *Reading and learning from text.* New York: Erlbaum.

Sizer, T. (1984). *Horace's compromise: The dilemma of the American high school.* Boston: Houghton Mifflin.

Sizer, T. (1992). *Horace's school: Redesigning the American high school.* Boston: Houghton Mifflin.

Smith, F. (1985). *Reading without nonsense* (2nd ed.). New York: Teachers College Press.

Smith, F. (1988). *Joining the literacy club.* Portsmouth, NH: Heinemann.

Strunk, W., & White, E. B. (2000). *The elements of style* (4th ed.). Boston: Allyn & Bacon.

Tharp, R., & Gallimore, R. (1989). Rousing schools to life. *American Educator: The Professional Journal of the American Federation of Teachers, 13,* 20–25.

Tovani, C. (2000). *I read it but I don't get it: Comprehension strategies for adolescent readers.* Portland, ME: Stenhouse.

Vacca, R. T., & Alvermann, D. E. (1998). The crisis in adolescent literacy: Is it real or imagined? *NASSP Bulletin, 82*(600), 4–9.

Vacca, R., & Vacca, J. (2002). *Content area reading: Literacy and learning across the curriculum* (7th ed.). Boston: Allyn & Bacon.

Vygotsky, L. (1978). *Mind in society: The development of higher psychological processes.* Cambridge, MA: MIT Press.

Wasik, B. (1998). Using volunteers as reading tutors: Guidelines for successful practices. *The Reading Teacher, 51,* 562–570.

Weaver, C. (1996). *Teaching grammar in context.* Portsmouth, NH: Heinemann.

Wilde. S. (1992). *You kan red this: Spelling and punctuation for whole language classrooms K–6.* Portsmouth, NH: Heinemann.

Winograd, P. (1984). Strategic difficulties in summarizing texts. *Reading Research Quarterly, 19,* 404–425.

Worthy, J., Broaddus, K., & Ivey, G. (2001). *Pathways to independence: Reading, writing, and learning in grades 3–8.* New York: Guilford Press.

Worthy, J., Moorman, M., & Turner, M. (1999). What Johnny likes to read is hard to find in school. *Reading Research Quarterly, 34,* 12–27.

Zemelman, S., Daniels, H., & Hyde, A. (1998). *Best practice: New standards for teaching and learning in America's schools* (2nd ed). Portsmouth, NH: Heinemann.

Zirinsky, D., & Rau, S. (2001). *A classroom of teenaged readers: Nurturing reading processes in senior high English.* New York: Longman.

Children's/Trade Books

Adoff, A. (1990). *Sports pages.* New York: HarperCollins.

Anderson, J. (2000). *Rookie: Tamika Whitmore's first year in the WBNA.* New York: Dutton.

Ardley, N. (2000). *Eyewitness: Music.* London: Dorling Kindersley.

Base, G. (1987). *Animalia.* New York: Harry N. Abrams.

Bingham, J. (1999). *Usborne world history: Medieval times.* Newmarket, Ontario, Canada: Usborne.

Brashares, A. (2001). *The sisterhood of the traveling pants.* New York: Delacorte.

Bridges, R. (1999). *Through my eyes.* New York: Scholastic.

Brown, T. (1998). *Tom Brown's field guide to nature observation and tracking.* New York: Berkley.

Burg, A. E. (2003). *E is for empire: A New York state alphabet.* Chelsea, MI: Sleeping Bear Press.

Burleigh, R. (2001). *Hoops.* New York: Voyager.

Coles, R. (1995). *The story of Ruby Bridges.* New York: Scholastic.

Colman, P. (1995). *Toilets, bathtubs, sinks, and sewers: A history of the bathroom.* New York: Atheneum.

Colman, P. (1995). *Rosie the riveter: Women working on the home front in World War II.* New York: Crown.

Dawkins, R. (2003). *Best American science and nature writing 2003.* Boston: Houghton Mifflin.

Franco, B. (Ed.). (2001). *You hear me?: Poems and writing by teenage boys.* Cambridge, MA: Candlewick Press.

Gilson, J. (1992). *Hello, my name is Scrambled Eggs.* New York: Aladdin.

Golenbock, P. (1990). *Teammates.* San Diego, CA: Harcourt Brace Jovanovich.

Greenaway, T. (2000). *The water cycle.* New York: Raintree.

Haskins, J. (2000). *One nation under a groove: Rap music and its roots.* New York: Jump at the Sun.

Herzog, B. (2004). *H is for home run: A baseball alphabet.* Chelsea, MI: Sleeping Bear Press.

Hunt, J. (1989). *Illuminations: A medieval alphabet book.* New York: Bradbury.

Hunter, S. (1996). *The unbreakable code.* Flagstaff, AZ: Northland.

Innocenti, R. (1991). *Rose Blanche.* New York: Stewart, Tabori & Chang.

Isadora, R. (1991). *Ben's trumpet.* New York: HarperTrophy.

Jackson, D. (1996). *The bone detectives: How forensic anthropologists solve crimes and uncover mysteries of the dead.* Boston: Little, Brown.

Jenkins, S. (2002). *Life on earth: The story of evolution.* Boston: Houghton Mifflin.

Jenkins, S. (2002). *Top of the world: Climbing Mount Everest.* New York: Turtleback.

Jones, C. F. (1991). *Mistakes that worked.* New York: Doubleday.

Krakauer, J. (1997). *Into thin air: A personal account of the Mount Everest disaster.* New York: Villard.

Manchester Medieval Portal. Manchester, UK: Manchester University Press. Available online at *www.medievalsources.co.uk*

Myers, W. D. (1999). *Monster.* New York: HarperCollins.

Pallotta, J. (1996). *The freshwater alphabet book.* New York: Charlesbridge.

Paulsen, G. (1995). *Winterdance: The fine madness of running the Iditarod.* New York: Harvest.

Polacco, P. (1998). *Thank you, Mr. Falker.* New York: Philomel Books.

Raschka, C. (1992). *Charlie Parker played bebop.* New York: Orchard Books.

Ryan, P. M. (2000). *Esperanza rising.* New York: Scholastic.

Schlosser, E. (2002). *Fast food nation: The dark side of the All-American meal.* New York: Perennial.

Speare, E. G. (1972). *The witch of blackbird pond.* New York: Bantam Doubleday Dell.

Stanley, J. (1992). *Children of the dust bowl: The true story of the school at Weedpatch Camp.* New York: Trumpet.

Tallchief, M., & Wells, R. (2001). *Tallchief: America's prima ballerina.* New York: Puffin.

Tsuchiya, Y. (1988). *The faithful elephants.* New York: Houghton Mifflin.

Uchida, Y. (1993). *The bracelet.* New York: Philomel Books.

Wick, W. (1997). *A drop of water: A book of science and wonder.* New York: Scholastic.

Wilks, M. (1986). *The ultimate alphabet book.* New York: Henry Holt.

Index

Page numbers followed by an *f* indicate figure.

176

Index